The Humility Advantage

The Humility Advantage

When doubt becomes wisdom and humility becomes strength

Revealing the leader within

J. Alexander

The Humility Advantage
Joseph Alexander

All rights reserved
Copyright © 2026 by Joseph Alexander

No part of this publication may be reproduced, distributed, or transmitted in any form or by any means, including photocopying, recording, or other electronic or mechanical methods, without the prior written permission of the publisher, except in the case of brief quotations embodied in critical reviews and certain other noncommercial uses permitted by copyright law.

Published by Spines
ISBN 979-8-90222-562-1

Contents

About the Foreword	vii
Foreword for The Humility Advantage	ix
Preface	xi
Dedication	xv
Introduction	1
Reading This Book Won't Change You—But Using It Might	

Part I: The Inner War

1. Uncovering the Gold Within — 15
   The Invisible Battle—What Imposter Syndrome Costs High Performers
2. The Cost of the Mask — 33
   The armor that protected you is now the weight that's holding you back.
3. The False Self—When Modesty Is Just Self-Doubt in Disguise — 45
   The most dangerous lies are the ones we mistake for virtue.
4. Unmasking the Inner Critic — 57
   The most dangerous voice in leadership is rarely the loudest one in the room. It's the quiet one in your own head.

Part II: Reclaiming Your Power

5. Humility Rewired—Building Strength from the Inside Out — 75
   Humility is often misunderstood as weakness. In truth, it is one of the most neurologically and relationally powerful states a leader can cultivate.
6. Rewriting the Script—Tools to Reclaim Your Voice — 91
   Every leader carries a script—an internal narrative about who they are, how much they belong, and what they're allowed to say. The question is: who wrote yours?

7. Centered Leadership—Wisdom Over Wounds — 109
When leaders are praised for being "centered," what people are really noticing is stability under pressure.

8. Quiet Confidence—How to Speak Up Without Arrogance or Shrinking — 121
Most leaders swing between two extremes: shrinking when uncertain, posturing when pressured. But the highest-performing leaders live in a different zone altogether.

Part III: Leadership from the Center

9. Building Resilient Teams with Emotional Clarity — 139
Resilience is no longer a "nice-to-have" in leadership—it's the price of survival.

10. The Courage to Decide—How Humility Fuels Bold Decisions — 149
Every day, leaders face choices that affect not just projects and profits but people, cultures, and futures. The paradox is that humility—not bravado—is the key to bold decisions.

Part IV: The Legacy of a Humble Leader

11. Faith, Identity, and Eternal Impact — 165
The measure of a leader is not taken in the noise of the moment, but in the echoes that remain when their voice has gone silent.

12. The Daily Practice of Humble Confidence — 189
Confidence without humility turns brittle. Humility without confidence collapses into self-erasure. The leaders who endure are those who cultivate humble confidence—the capacity to walk into high-stakes moments grounded, steady, and open.

CONCLUSION — 199
You Were Never a Fraud—You Were Becoming a Leader

Afterword — 211

APPENDIX A: Complete Exercise Index — 213

APPENDIX B: QR Codes — 257

Citations — 259

About the Author — 267

About the Foreword

Thomas Blackwell: Leadership voice and language transformation expert

Thomas Blackwell is the CEO and Founder of Say Do Achieve and an international inspirational speaker who has delivered over 1,000 talks and workshops worldwide since beginning his speaking career in 2004. His expertise in transforming communication and mindset makes him a credible voice on leadership, having worked with corporations, executives, entrepreneurs, athletes, and students across multiple continents. His best-selling book, The Liberty of Our Language Revealed: We Bring About What We Talk About (2018), encapsulates his philosophy that words shape reality and results.

One of the highlights of my career is when I get to share the stage with Thomas. I am 12 years his senior, but when I grow up, I want to be like him.

You can get his book at **ThomasBlackwellSpeak.com**

Foreword for The Humility Advantage
By Thomas Blackwell

When I first met J. Alexander, my initial impression was simply, here's a guy that is confident of where he is going. His language and demeanor gave no room for doubt that he had a BIG IDEA and was going to accomplish it without anyone standing in his way. Then, as I have had personal conversations and interactions in different settings with J., I recognized a different and more elite level of confidence he clearly possesses. I call it Humble Confidence.

J. has a lot to offer, and you will easily discover that as you implement at any level the very detailed and researched framework of achieving The Humility Advantage. J. is the perfect qualified person to serve the world with this progressive methodology, because he himself has recognized the power of it in his own life. Therefore, it changes from a theory to a sure thing when implemented.

As J. states, this book, workbook, and inspirational dialogue will make a difference if and when you do the work. The very essence of that thought just stated requires what the book is all about, Humility!

It takes humility to recognize we need help and improvement in multiple areas of our lives. It takes humility to admit,

Foreword for The Humility Advantage

maybe we are not giving our best effort. It takes humility to write a book about the very subject.

Somewhere along the line, we have been taught that accepting compliments for a job well done or an achievement in some area of our lives merits us not being humble. I have proven the opposite to be true – accepting compliments is the best way to demonstrate Humble Gratitude. That being said, I openly compliment J. Alexander for having the Humble Courage to create this book and teach us how we can all be blessed by The Humility Advantage.

Sincerely,
Thomas Blackwell – CEO of Say Do Achieve

Preface

The Gold Buddha and the Clay Armor

Christine had always felt like a fake. Even though she was now the youngest team leader at her hospital, she spent every day worried that someone would discover she didn't really know what she was doing....even though she did. She called herself a leader, but inside, she felt like a scared kid pretending to be a grown-up.

One day, her mentor, Dr. Chen, noticed Christine sitting alone after a tough meeting. "You look like you're carrying the weight of the world," he said.

"I just... I don't think I'm cut out for this," Christine admitted. "Everyone else seems so confident. I'm just faking it."

Dr. Chen smiled. "Let me tell you a story about a gold Buddha."

He explained that in Thailand, there was once a huge clay Buddha statue. For hundreds of years, everyone thought it was just made of clay—nothing special. But one day, a piece of the clay cracked off. Underneath, they discovered the statue was made of solid gold! The clay had just been covering it up to protect it.

Preface

"You're like that Buddha," Dr. Chen said. "You were born gold—full of natural leadership ability. But as you grew up, you added layers of clay to protect yourself. You learned to doubt yourself, to hide your real thoughts, to act like someone you're not. Now that clay is getting in your way."

Christine thought about this. It was true—she spent so much energy trying to act like the 'perfect leader' that she exhausted herself. She never shared when she was uncertain. She never asked for help. She pretended to have all the answers.

"So how do I chip away the clay?" she asked.

Dr. Chen taught her something called the Daily Centering practice. Every morning, Christine would sit quietly for just ten minutes. She'd breathe slowly and pay attention to what was happening inside her—her worries, her feelings, her real thoughts. It felt weird at first, like she was wasting time. But slowly, something started to change.

Christine began to notice the difference between her real self and the character she'd been playing. The real Christine cared deeply about her patients. The character she played just worried about looking smart. The real Christine had good instincts about people. The character she played ignored those instincts and tried to follow some imaginary rulebook.

As Christine practiced more, she started making small changes. In meetings, when she didn't understand something, she said, "Can you explain that more? I want to make sure I get it right." At first, she thought people would think she was dumb. Instead, three other people said, "Oh, good, I was confused too!"

Preface

She started something called "leadership check-ins" with her team. Once a week, she'd ask, "What's one thing going well? What's one thing we could do better?" She wasn't pretending to be perfect anymore—she was being real.

Her team noticed. "Christine, you seem different lately," her colleague James said. "More... I don't know... more like yourself?"

"I'm trying to lead from the center," Christine explained. "Instead of trying to be some perfect leader from a textbook, I'm leading from who I really am—doubts and all."

The funny thing was, the more Christine admitted what she didn't know, the more her team trusted her. The more she showed her real feelings, the more her team felt safe sharing theirs. When she made a mistake and said, "I messed that up, here's what I learned," her team felt brave enough to try new things without fear.

One day, Christine faced her biggest challenge yet. The hospital was changing how all the teams worked, and her team was scared. The old Christine would have pretended she had everything figured out and forced everyone to smile and go along with it.

Instead, the new Christine gathered her team. "I know this change is scary," she said. "I'm scared too. But here's what I know: we're good at working together. We care about our patients. And we'll figure this out the same way we always do—by being honest with each other and helping each other out."

She didn't have a perfect plan. She didn't have all the answers. But she had something better—she had the courage to be real.

Preface

Her team pulled together. They helped each other through the tough transition. And when they succeeded, Christine realized something amazing: she'd been a good leader all along. She just had to stop covering up her gold with clay.

Years later, when Christine mentored young leaders herself, she told them Dr. Chen's story about the gold Buddha. "You don't need to become a great leader," she'd say. "You just need to stop pretending to be something you're not. Chip away the clay. Let your gold shine through."

And whenever a young leader said, "But I don't feel confident enough," Christine would smile and reply, "Good. That means you're humble enough to keep learning. Now, let me teach you about Daily Centering..."

The End... and Your Beginning

Christine's story is your story too. You were born gold, and life added clay. Are you ready to chip away at your clay?

Dedication

As weird, selfish, or arrogant as this may sound, I dedicate this book to me. I joke that humility is my greatest strength, but the truth is I need this book as much as anyone. When you chisel away my layers, you'll find woven into my character the antithesis of humility - pride. I want to overcome my pride, and I genuinely want to help people overcome their pride, and I believe the cure is humility - confident humility. Sounds like a contradiction, but as you read (and do the exercises), you'll find that they go hand in hand.

This book, then, is both a "how to" and my journey—my roadmap to becoming great and powerful through humility, like the greats below.

The greats, I've found, all shared one trait: humility.

Spiritual & Religious Leaders

• Mother Teresa – Lived among the poorest of the poor in Calcutta, serving with simplicity and love.

• St. Francis of Assisi – Renounced wealth and status to live a life of poverty, service, and humility.

• The Dalai Lama – Revered for his compassion, gentleness, and humble approach to leadership.

Dedication

- Desmond Tutu – South African archbishop who combined justice with humility and forgiveness during apartheid.

- David O. McKay – Remembered for his gentle spirit and Christlike demeanor, often teaching that "every member is a missionary."

- Gordon B. Hinckley – Despite presiding over tremendous growth in the Church of Jesus Christ of Latter-day Saints, he carried a warm, approachable, and humble tone, often using humor to put others at ease.

Political & Social Leaders

- Mahatma Gandhi – Led India's independence movement with simplicity, fasting, and servant-leadership.

- Abraham Lincoln – Known for his modesty, openness to criticism, and deep empathy in leadership.

- Nelson Mandela – After decades in prison, he returned with forgiveness and humility rather than revenge.

Innovators & Thinkers

- Albert Schweitzer – Philosopher, physician, and humanitarian who gave up prestige to serve in Africa.

- Fred Rogers (Mister Rogers) – Brought kindness, humility, and empathy to generations through children's television.

- Albert Einstein – Despite his genius, he often downplayed his brilliance and acknowledged his limits.

Dedication

Business & Leadership

• Herb Kelleher (founder of Southwest Airlines) – Known for humility, servant leadership, and putting employees first.

• Jim Collins' "Level 5 Leaders" (concept, but modeled after real executives) – Leaders who blend humility with fierce resolve.

Yet all these remarkable people would point beyond themselves.

None of them even compares to my Master, Friend, and Savior, Jesus Christ. My life is a constant quest to be more like Him. And I slip up every day.

Introduction
Reading This Book Won't Change You—But Using It Might

You've read books on leadership before-maybe dozens. You underline passages, nod along, feel inspired for a few days, and then lapse back into your default patterns. The insights faded. The habits didn't "stick." You're still the same leader, just with a shelf full of good ideas you don't actually use.

This book will be the same, unless you use it differently.

And though *The Humility Advantage* will inform you and probably even entertain you, it's actually written with one intention in mind: to *interrupt* you. To cause friction between who you are today and who you're designed to be. But friction alone doesn't build anything. You need a method to convert insight into practice, and practice into character.

This is a Workbook Masquerading as a Book

Here's how to use it to make a permanent change:

1. Read with a pen, not a highlighter

Highlighting is passive. It gives the illusion of involvement without requiring anything from you in return. Instead, as you go through each chapter, have with you a **journal** or notebook with three columns:

- **Recognition:** What pattern in this chapter do I recognize in myself? Be specific. Not "I sometimes lack humility," but "Last Tuesday, when my CFO challenged my budget assumptions, I felt my jaw tighten, and I interrupted her twice."

- **Resistance:** What did I find myself reading in this chapter and saying, No, that's just not how it is? What sentence or idea set me off? Resistance is data. It often points to the growth edge you most need.

- **Commitment:** What is *one* micro-practice I will test this week? Not five. One. Make it so small it feels almost trivial. "I will pause for three breaths before responding in my Thursday leadership team meeting."

If you are done with a chapter without writing in all three columns, you didn't read it; you skimmed it.

2. The exercises are optional—but transformation isn't

Throughout this book, you'll encounter dozens of exercises, reflections, and practices designed to move you from insight to action. Some will be brief self-assessments. Others will be challenging 30-day experiments. A few will require feedback from your team or trusted colleagues.

You don't have to do every exercise. In fact, you don't have to do any of them. Some readers learn through reflection alone. Others need to take action to internalize concepts. You know your learning style better than I do. But if you do one exercise, make it journaling. It's a lost art. Our generation has gotten lazy about it, yet journaling forces reflection in a way nothing else does. And I mean pen and paper—old school. There's real neurological benefit to writing things down by hand.

Now, I'm all about technology. So after you write it, feel free to dictate it into a journaling app. That way, you get both the brain benefits of handwriting and a digital backup for posterity (which matters to me—maybe to you too).

But here's the truth: reading about humility doesn't make you humble any more than reading about fitness makes you strong. If you want lasting change—not just temporary inspiration—you need to do *something* beyond reading.

If you're unsure where to begin, or if you want to create your own course in development, refer to Appendix A: Exercise Summary. In it, I have listed each of the exercises in the book by category—ego work, feedback practices, team leadership, self-awareness, and consistency building. Browse the list. Take note of which exercises strike you as, "I should do that someday." Do those now. The ones you're resisting are generally the ones you need most.

You might use Appendix A in several ways:

- **The Focused Path:** Pick 5-7 exercises that address your most urgent growth edge and commit to completing them over 90 days.
- **The Deep Dive:** Choose exercises from a single theme (like ego work or feedback practices) and spend a quarter becoming exceptional in that domain.

- **The Team Curriculum:** Select exercises designed for group reflection and use them as the backbone of your leadership team's development.
- **The Intuitive Approach:** Read straight through, try whatever resonates in the moment, and reference Appendix A later when you're ready for more structured practice.

The method matters less than the honesty. Don't fool yourself into thinking that reading alone will change you. It won't. But deliberate practice—even just a few well-chosen exercises—can rewire decades of reactive patterns.

3. The Science Is There If You Want It—Skip It If You Don't

Throughout this book, you'll encounter research citations, neuroscience explanations, and evidence from organizational behavior studies. Some readers find these grounding—they want to know *why* the practices work, not just *that* they work. If that's you, the science will reinforce your commitment.

But if you're the kind of leader who thinks, "Just tell me what to do, and I'll try it," skip those sections entirely. The practices work whether you understand the prefrontal cortex or not. What matters is that you *use* them, not that you can explain the mechanism behind them. Trust your experience over the data if that's how you're wired.

4. Center Yourself: Make "The Centered Leader's Playbook" your OS

At the end of several chapters, you'll find tactical practices: daily centering, wisdom journaling, feedback rituals, consistency audits, non-attachment checks, and team reflections. These are not recommendations. They are the infrastructure for the change.

Take on *one* practice and complete 30 days before taking on another. Not because you're slow, but because lasting change is built through repetition, not accumulation. A single practice done daily for a month rewires your nervous system. Six practices done sporadically for a week do nothing.

Begin with Daily Centering. It is the bedrock, and all other practices are easier when you start each day anchored rather than reacting.

To "center" means to pause and bring your attention inward—often with a few slow, intentional breaths—so you begin your study focused, calm, and present, rather than swept up by distractions or stress. It can be as simple as sitting quietly for one minute, feeling your breath, and noticing the sensations in your body.

5. Find an accountability structure—or this book will become decoration

Behavior change dies in isolation. You need witnesses. Before you complete reading this introduction, choose one of these structures:

Option A Partner for Weekly Review

Find one peer, just one-a colleague, a friend, a fellow leader-who also buys into growth. Every Friday at noon, you each send a three-sentence text:

- One pattern I saw this week
- One habit I kept (or broke)
- One question I am carrying into next week

That is it-no meetings, no hour-long debriefs. Just accountability that takes 90 seconds.

Option B: The Group Lab

If you're leading a team, make this book the curriculum for your leadership development. At the end of every staff meeting, take five minutes to explore one practice from the playbook. Rotate who facilitates. Make your team the laboratory in which you test these ideas together. The vulnerability you model will permit them to grow alongside you.

Option C: The Monthly Audit

Set a recurring calendar reminder on the first of each month: "Humility Audit." Block 20 minutes. Rereading Recognition, Resistance, and Commitment entries from your journal during the last 30 days. Ask yourself: *What actually changed? Where did I revert to old patterns? What practice needs to be reinforced or replaced?*

The Humility Advantage

Without one of these structures, you will read this book, feel temporarily inspired, and change nothing.

6. Discomfort expected—that's the curriculum.

If you feel you're reading this book comfortably, you're doing it wrong. Humility isn't a feel-good concept; it is a practice that means seeing yourself clearly, including those parts with which you've been in avoidance. You will come across chapters that expose your ego defenses and name your wound-driven scripts, revealing the gap between your self-image and your real-world impact.

Good. That's the price of admission to real leadership.

And when you come to a chapter where you just think you should close the book, well, that's the chapter to reread. And if there's an exercise that is too vulnerable to do, just know that's the most growth-filled exercise that's out there. Your resistance is a map. Follow it.

7. This is not a book to finish; this is a book to return to

You'll want to read this straight through in a few sittings. Don't. This is not a novel. It's a field manual.

Read one chapter. Live with it for a week. Journal on it. Try the practice. Notice what shifts—and doesn't. Then move to the next chapter.

When you reach the end, you won't be done. You will be ready to start again, because you will be reading different words as a different leader. I know this because I had to learn it myself: I used to read dozens of books per year. Then I realized I was being entertained by them but not transforming. So I decided to read just a few books a year and really learn and understand what they were saying. Let this be one of those books.

The chapter on ego, which felt abstract in your first pass, will land viscerally when you reread it six months later, after you have watched yourself defend a bad decision in a board meeting. The section on nonattachment that seemed so simple will reveal new layers after you have experienced how praise can inflate you and criticism can crush you.

This book is designed for re-entry. The insights compound. And when you return to it six months or a year from now, Appendix A will help you quickly locate the exercises that address whatever new challenge you're facing.

8. Measure What Matters: Impact Not Intention

At the end of 90 days, don't ask yourself, "Did I read the book?" or even "Did I do the exercises?" Ask: "Did anything change in how I lead?"

Better yet, ask your team. Use the Consistency Audit from Chapter 7: "Do I show up the same in pressure as in calm?" If they say yes, and you were reactive before, nothing changed. If they say, "You seem more grounded lately," or "You've been listening more," or "You acknowledged your blind spot in that meeting"-that's evidence.

Leadership presence is not self-reported; it's witnessed. If your team isn't seeing different, different didn't happen.

9. Repetition on purpose

As you read, you'll encounter key concepts multiple times, each from a different vantage point. This isn't accidental. Real change doesn't happen through a single exposure to an idea—it happens through repeated engagement that allows us to see the same truth in new ways and integrate it more deeply into our practice.

When you encounter a familiar concept in a new chapter, resist the urge to skip ahead. Instead, pause and ask yourself: "What am I noticing about this idea now that I didn't see before?" Write that insight in your journal. The repetition isn't redundancy—it's your brain building new neural pathways. Each time you revisit a concept, you're integrating it at a deeper level, moving it from intellectual understanding to embodied practice.

A Final Word Before You Get Started

Humility is not self-deprecation or false modesty. It's the strength to see yourself clearly, admit what you don't know, and remain open to being wrong. It's the capacity to lead without needing to dominate, to listen without needing to defend, and to grow without needing to pretend you've arrived.

The leaders who truly model this-the ones to whom people feel attracted, whom they go to and remember-are not those who are loud or smooth but those who have done the heavy lifting of becoming honest with themselves first. This book will not make you one of them, but the practices and exercises inside it can, if you let them interrupt you, humble you, reshape you.

Now, before you turn the page:

- Which accountability structure will you choose? Write it down. Text that person. Set that calendar reminder right now.
- Commit to reading with a pen, not a highlighter. Keep your three-column journal (Recognition, Resistance, Commitment) beside you.
- Promise yourself you'll complete at least one exercise per chapter before moving forward.

When you're ready to design a more structured development path, Appendix A catalogs every exercise by theme. But for now, just start with Chapter 1—and actually do the work it asks of you.

Because if you don't commit to a structure now, this book will end up on your shelf next to all the others—full of good ideas you never used.

Let's begin.

Before you begin....

Download your workbook and take the humility assessment—so you identify your starting point.

Get the Companion Workbook - Free 🔼

Take the Humility Assessment - Free 🔼

Part I: The Inner War

Chapter 1
Uncovering the Gold Within
The Invisible Battle—What Imposter Syndrome Costs High Performers

---

You're not alone. You're just wearing armor that no longer fits.

In 1957, a group of monks at Wat Traimit Temple in Bangkok prepared to relocate a large Buddha statue. The image was over ten feet tall, weighed several tons, and—by all appearances—was made of plain stucco. During the move, the rigging slipped, and the statue fell, cracking the surface. A glint flashed from the fracture. The monks chipped cautiously at the outer coating and uncovered one of modern Buddhism's most surprising discoveries: a solid gold statue that had been disguised centuries earlier to protect it from invading armies. Over generations, the disguise became the identity—until a fracture revealed the truth beneath.

Leadership works the same way. We learn to protect ourselves early: speak with certainty, hide the doubts, outperform the room, and never let anyone see the seams. The habits that shielded us in high-pressure environments become the persona we carry. Eventually, the disguise becomes the identity. And like the monks before the crack, we bow to a version of ourselves that isn't the real thing.

The Armor We Wear

Let's name the layers most leaders use as armor:

- **Relentless achievement** to outrun the fear of not being enough
- **Perfectionism and positional authority** to compensate for uncertainty
- **Credentials and bravado** to keep imposter feelings out of sight

Those layers work—until they don't. In coaching rooms and boardrooms, the same confessions surface: "I'm waiting to be found out." "I keep winning, but it never feels like enough." "I can't relax; I have to prove it again tomorrow."

That voice has a label—**imposter syndrome**—and it's far more common than most leaders admit.

A Silent Epidemic

A comprehensive meta-analysis by Bravata et al. (2020), published in the *Journal of General Internal Medicine*, reviewed 62 studies and found that **9% to 82%** of people experience imposter syndrome at some point in their careers. Translation: this is not rare, and it's not about "weak" people. It's a predictable by-product of high-stakes environments.

Imposter thoughts change how leaders behave in the moments that matter. Research links them with higher anxiety and depression, and with behavioral patterns that hurt performance: risk-avoidance, under-delegation, and chronic overwork. That's not a personality quirk—it's a **leadership tax** that compounds over time.

If you're burning energy proving your right to be in the room, you're not using that energy to see farther, serve deeper, or build people.

Here's the uncomfortable truth: **survival strategies don't scale.** The same habits that got you through the chaos—hyper-control, constant proving, neatly stage-managed certainty—will eventually choke learning, trust, and innovation. The clay hardens; the gold stops shining.

Behind the Smile: A Story from the Corps

My first summer at the United States Marine Corps Officer Candidate School, I finished near the bottom. The next summer, I finished near the top. At The Basic School (TBS)—training for all Marine Corps lieutenants—I finished near the bottom again. I found myself as a supply officer in an infantry battalion, surrounded by warriors who seemed to belong in a way I didn't. I wasn't dumb. But as I was *taking* all the different evaluations—written tests, combat simulations, leadership assessments—the voices in my head telling me I shouldn't be there *were* a massive distraction. It led to anxiety I couldn't name and didn't dare admit. I remember standing in my battalion commander's office one afternoon, wondering why the room was spinning. I couldn't tell anyone the room was spinning. What would they think? I was covered with clay, and I couldn't find the gold within. Years later, I'd learn that my experience wasn't unique—it was textbook imposter syndrome playing out in woodland camouflage. This is the cruel paradox of imposter syndrome: the more you succeed, the less you trust the success.

What's Under Your Clay?

If you're like most high achievers, the armor started as something noble: a commitment to excellence, a refusal to be mediocre, a promise to protect your people. Over time, that promise calcified into self-pressure and performance theater. You built a persona that always has an answer, never needs help, and treats doubt as a threat.

It worked—until the weight of holding it together began to cost more than it returned.

Check yourself on a few telltale behaviors:

- You default to certainty in meetings, even when you're only 60% sure
- You keep "quick wins" for yourself and delegate the messy, visible work reluctantly
- You delay hard feedback because you fear the backlash—or the exposure
- You hear dissent as disrespect instead of data

If any of that lands, good. Cracks are invitations. The question isn't "Am I a fraud?" The question is "Am I willing to chip away what no longer serves the mission?"

A True Story About the Cost of Armor

Psychologist Amy Edmondson's foundational research on psychological safety—the belief that a team is safe for

The Humility Advantage

interpersonal risk-taking—explains why armored leadership backfires. In a landmark field study across real hospital teams, Edmondson showed that groups with higher psychological safety reported **more** errors—not because they made more mistakes, but because they felt safe enough to speak up about them. Teams that feared blame reported less and learned less.

In complex systems (read: every modern organization), silent teams are fragile teams.

The leadership implication is clear: when I'm defending my image, I punish uncertainty—my own and others'. People quickly learn to keep their heads down. Problems go underground. The status report looks green; reality is red. Leaders mistake compliance for alignment, and quiet for confidence.

Consider the **Michigan Keystone ICU Project**. Clinicians implemented a simple evidence-based bundle—hand hygiene, sterile barrier precautions, and a central-line insertion checklist—paired with a culture shift that normalized speaking up. The result? A dramatic reduction in catheter-related bloodstream infections, with some reports citing reductions on the order of two-thirds.

Humility—manifested as checklists, team voice, and willingness to be corrected—**saved lives**.

That's the paradox of high performance: the more responsibility you carry, the less you can afford ego-protected leadership. Outcomes ride on information flow. And information only flows in cultures where people can say what is true without fear.

The Doctor Behind the Mask

Dr. Suzanne Koven was a highly respected physician at Massachusetts General Hospital and a faculty member at Harvard Medical School. Her credentials were impeccable. She had trained at top institutions, published articles, and mentored young doctors.

But behind the accolades was a persistent internal whisper: *"I am a fraud."*

In a letter published in the *New England Journal of Medicine*, Dr. Koven confessed that throughout her career—even after becoming an attending physician—she felt like she didn't truly belong. Each accomplishment was accompanied by the gnawing fear that someone would eventually figure out she wasn't as capable as they thought.

It wasn't that she lacked confidence in her clinical skills. It was the quiet belief that her worth was conditional—that if she stopped overachieving, she would stop being valuable.

It wasn't until years later, through reflection and conversations with other women in medicine, that she began to see the truth: She was never a fraud. She was just exhausted from trying to earn a sense of belonging she already deserved.

Today, Dr. Koven speaks openly about imposter syndrome in medicine. She encourages young physicians to understand that true humility doesn't mean doubting your worth—it means knowing it deeply enough that you no longer need to prove it.

The Role of Culture and Identity

For marginalized and underrepresented professionals, imposter syndrome often runs deeper—and cuts sharper.

A 2021 study published in the *Journal of Vocational Behavior* found that **people of color, first-generation professionals, and women in male-dominated fields** reported higher levels of imposter feelings. These weren't just psychological patterns—they were reactions to real systemic barriers and exclusionary work cultures.

"When you're the only one in the room who looks like you, it doesn't feel like imposter syndrome. It feels like survival."
— *Monique, Latina VP in finance*

Rafael, the first in his family to attend college, became a tenure-track professor at a top-tier university. On paper, it was the American Dream. But inside, he felt like he was constantly auditioning. "Everyone else seems fluent in this hidden language. I still second-guess whether I used the right fork at faculty dinners."

His imposter syndrome didn't come from incompetence—it came from **cultural dissonance**. The ivory tower was not built for people like him. It wasn't until he connected with other first-generation academics that he found peace in his presence.

Imposter syndrome in these cases is not a distortion—it's a response to **invalidating environments**. To address it, we must expand the frame from internal to systemic.

The Neuroscience and Evidence for a Different Way

Imposter syndrome isn't just emotional—it's physiological. Studies show that individuals experiencing imposter syndrome demonstrate distinct brain activity patterns: hyperactive amygdalas (processing threat where none exists), reduced prefrontal cortex function (impaired decision-making), and hypercritical default mode networks (reinforcing negative self-beliefs).

This creates a vicious cycle. Leaders with imposter syndrome may micromanage to compensate for self-doubt, over-prepare to avoid criticism, and withhold creative ideas out of fear of failure. This doesn't just stifle their growth—it creates a ripple effect across the team.

But leaders don't need more bravado; they need more emotional intelligence grounded in humility. A meta-analysis in the *Journal of Organizational Behavior* found that emotional intelligence shows a meaningful relationship with job performance beyond personality and cognitive ability. Leaders who can accurately read themselves and others, regulate emotion, and build high-trust interactions perform better—even after you account for IQ and traits.

Where does humility come in? **It's the operating posture that lets EQ actually work.** You cannot empathize if image management is your first priority. You cannot listen if you're addicted to being right. You cannot regulate your own affect if every question feels like an attack on your status.

The Nervous System of Leadership

Under stress, your nervous system narrows to threat management; you protect, control, and prove. That's why leaders who intend to be calm still snap, interrupt, and micromanage when the heat rises. Your intent matters less than your state.

Enter mindfulness—not as platitudes, but as a well-studied method for training attention and down-regulating reactivity. A large meta-analysis in *JAMA Internal Medicine* found that structured meditation programs produce small to moderate improvements in anxiety and depressive symptoms. That matters because a calmer baseline gives you access to better executive functions in the moment you need them.

Neuroimaging research adds another layer: participants in an eight-week mindfulness program showed gray-matter increases in brain regions tied to learning, emotion regulation, and perspective-taking—precisely the capacities leaders draw on to listen well, weigh tradeoffs, and choose their response.

Practical takeaway: Humility is easier to choose when your physiology isn't hijacked. The combination—humility + mindfulness—creates a leader who can notice defensiveness rising, name it internally, pause, and respond from purpose rather than protectiveness. That's not soft; it's disciplined.

What Humble, High-EQ Leadership Looks Like

If EQ is the tool and humility is the grip, behavior is the cutting edge. You don't need a personality transplant. You need repeatable moves:

1. Name uncertainty before it names you

"I'm 60% confident in this direction; here's the risk I might be missing." Watch how quickly the room improves your thinking when you make that safe.

2. Make dissent easy

"What would a smart critic say?" When people see you reward challenge instead of punishing it, they volunteer reality sooner. That's how you compress risk.

3. Use checklists for ego-heavy work

The Keystone ICU playbook wasn't about intelligence; it was about reliability, voice, and accountability. In your world, that might mean pre-mortems, decision logs, or red-team reviews. (A "pre-mortem" is a proactive risk assessment technique where a team imagines that a project or initiative has already failed, then works backward to identify all the possible reasons why it might have failed. This exercise helps surface hidden risks, assumptions, and potential weaknesses before the project begins, allowing teams to address them in advance and increase the chances of success).

4. Translate emotion into data

When a stakeholder is "difficult," ask, "What outcome are they protecting?" Emotional literacy turns conflict into information.

5. Close the loop publicly

Call out by name where someone's candor improved a decision. Safety spreads through stories of what gets praised as much as what gets punished.

The Mirror vs. the Armor

You've probably met both kinds of leaders:

Armor leaders fill the room; everything tightens around them. People watch the weather of their mood. Dissent gets coded as disloyalty. Everyone learns to play defense.

Mirror leaders bring clarity. They hold up a clean reflection: what is true, what matters, and what the team is capable of when fear isn't driving. People breathe. Output rises.

The difference isn't charisma or IQ. It's posture. Armor leaders personalize uncertainty and over-control. Mirror leaders normalize uncertainty and orchestrate learning. The former exhausts teams. The latter compounds the capability.

When Satya Nadella became CEO of Microsoft, he didn't win by out-muscling competitors; he shifted the culture from "know-it-all" to "learn-it-all," made empathy a leadership value, and opened the windows—collaboration up, walls down, results obvious. The mechanism is the point: **humility expands the system's ability to sense, learn, and adapt.**

But What About Credibility?

Leaders often resist humility because they fear it will undercut authority: "If I admit I don't know, I'll lose the room." The evidence suggests the opposite. Authentic leadership research shows that when leaders are self-aware, transparent, and values-consistent, trust increases—and with it, engagement and discretionary effort.

In medical settings, leader inclusiveness and psychological safety are associated with higher error reporting (which is what you want) and stronger learning climates. The appearance of invulnerability buys silence; authenticity buys the truth.

What Actually Helps: Evidence-Based Interventions

Research shows that with the right support and strategies, imposter syndrome can be significantly reduced—and even transformed into deeper leadership confidence.

Cognitive Behavioral Therapy (CBT)

CBT helps people identify, challenge, and replace distorted thinking patterns—especially black-and-white thinking, catastrophizing, and self-doubt. A 2020 study in the *Journal of Counseling Psychology* found that group-based CBT programs targeting imposter feelings led to significant reductions in imposter syndrome scores, along with gains in self-compassion and leadership confidence.

Executive Coaching and Group Reflection

A 2019 study in the *International Coaching Psychology Review* found that after 12 weeks of coaching, 76% of participants reported decreased imposter feelings and improved self-trust. Group coaching adds normalization—when leaders hear others echo their inner doubts, shame dissolves.

Mindfulness and Somatic Work

Imposter syndrome lives in the body. The tension in your jaw before a big presentation. The shallow breathing in a high-stakes meeting. Mind-body interventions help reduce this physiological stress and restore nervous system regulation.

Simple techniques: Box breathing (inhale 4, hold 4, exhale 4, hold 4). Grounding exercises. Body scanning. These restore calm and help reconnect your brain with your body—so you're not leading from adrenaline, but from alignment.

Narrative Coaching

This focuses on helping leaders rewrite the stories they tell themselves. Imposter syndrome clings to stories like "If I let up for a second, I'll fail" or "They only picked me because there was no one else." In narrative coaching, we ask: *Whose voice is that? When did you first learn that? What story do you want to live instead?*

Tools to Rewire Self-Perception

The Credibility Bank: Keep a running log of your accomplishments. For each, include what you did, why it mattered, and what strengths it required. This becomes your "bank account" of evidence when imposter thoughts arise.

The Reframe Ritual: When your inner critic says "I'm not qualified" or "That was just luck," respond with "I've done this before" and "I earned this opportunity." Repetition turns reframes into new beliefs.

The Reflected Best Self Exercise: Ask 5–10 people who know you well to describe a time when they saw you at your best. Identify common themes. This dismantles the lie of the imposter and replaces it with a real-time mirror.

A Practical Reset: From Performing to Revealing

If you're serious about chipping away the clay, here's a simple sequence you can implement this week:

1. Begin with state, not script.

Before a high-stakes interaction, take 90 seconds of quiet. Watch your breath. If your chest is tight and your jaw is set, don't power through. Lengthen the exhale and drop your shoulders.

2. Lead with context and uncertainty. In meetings:

"Here's what we know; here's what's ambiguous; here's where I need your judgment." You've just enabled better data in five minutes than most teams see in a month.

3. Invite one clarifying challenge.

"What are we missing that could bite us later?" Call on voices you don't usually hear. Reward the candor.

4. Decide, then document the learning.

Record assumptions, owners, and next checks. This is humility in operational form.

5. Close the loop with gratitude.

Name how someone's input improved the decision. You're teaching what gets status: not being right, making us righter.

The Crack Is the Start

You don't need to shatter your identity to find your gold. You need a crack—an honest moment where the shine of something truer peeks through the clay. For many leaders, that moment is forced by exhaustion or a near-miss. Choose a different path. Initiate your own fracture:

- Admit one thing you don't know—in public
- Ask one person you intimidate, "What's one thing I do that makes your job harder?" Then listen
- Replace one monologue with a map of uncertainty and a request for insight

This is not about being "nice." It's about being accurate. High-stakes systems reward leaders who see reality sooner and mobilize people faster. Humility is the speed hack because it removes the cognitive overhead of protecting an image.

The monks at Wat Traimit didn't create the gold; they just uncovered it. Likewise, humility does not create your worth, competence, or authority. It reveals them. The clay had a purpose—protection in dangerous times. But once the threat passes, the disguise becomes the prison.

You Are Not a Fraud. You Are Becoming.

If no one has told you this before, let me be the first:

You're not a fraud. You're just growing.

The fear you feel is not a flaw—it's a sign that you're stretching. It's what happens when your external impact has outpaced your internal integration.

You can close the distance between who you seem to be and who you truly are. You can rewrite the story from survival to self-trust.

You are here on purpose. You've done the work—and you're still doing it.

The world doesn't need a perfect leader. It needs a *present* one. A *real* one. It needs *you*—not the mask, not the over-functioning version, not the high-achieving persona. Just you.

You're not faking it. **You're becoming it.**

Chapter Takeaway

Imposter syndrome isn't a flaw in your character. It's a call to examine the story you're telling yourself—and replace fear-based habits with aligned action.

But you cannot thrive if you are constantly at war with yourself. Your leadership cannot scale beyond your self-trust.

So give yourself permission to let go of the mask, the pressure, the fear of being "found out."

You are already found. You are already enough. You are already becoming the leader your work, your team, and your world need.

Reflection Prompt #1

Where are you operating from, plaster instead of gold? Name the behavior in a sentence that a direct report would recognize. Then decide the smallest, most public crack you're willing to make this week.

The Humility Advantage

In the chapters ahead, we'll move from why to how: translating humility, emotional intelligence, and mindful state control into concrete practices you can test in the next meeting, the next decision, and the next season of your leadership. For now, hold the image: a fracture, a glint, the steady work of chipping away. Not to become less—but to let more of the real leader within be seen.

Chapter 2
The Cost of the Mask
The armor that protected you is now the weight that's holding you back.

You can build an impressive career wearing armor. You can even get promoted for it. In fact, in many organizations, the armor is rewarded: decisive postures get praised, perfect presentations get promoted, and polished certainty is mistaken for competence.

But the mask extracts a cost. Always. It takes a toll physically, psychologically, and operationally. You can pay for it with health, with innovation, or with people. Sometimes with all three.

If Chapter 1 was the crack in the clay—the glimpse of gold beneath—then Chapter 2 is the x-ray. It shows us what the mask is doing beneath the surface and why the long-term price tag of performing leadership is one no organization can afford.

What the Mask Actually Costs

Let's start with scope.

The Bravata et al. (2020) systematic review we referenced in Chapter 1 examined 62 studies with 14,161 participants. The prevalence range—9% to 82%—tells us imposter thoughts are not rare, not gender-bound, and not a quirk. They are a predictable response in high-stakes systems.

Now the harder truth: the costs aren't only emotional.

- Among U.S. physicians, a large national study in *Mayo Clinic Proceedings* found imposter experiences were independently associated with higher burnout, more suicidal ideation, and lower professional fulfillment. That's not soft stuff. That's medical errors, malpractice risk, and hundreds of thousands in turnover and replacement costs.
- In corporate sectors, imposter feelings correlate with weaker motivation to lead, lower job satisfaction, and decreased organizational citizenship behaviors—the discretionary acts that fuel innovation and teamwork.
- A 2019 *Frontiers in Psychology* study across multiple industries found that employees with strong imposter tendencies were significantly less likely to pursue promotion opportunities even when their performance reviews qualified them. Potential stayed locked inside.

In medical education—a useful proxy for any elite training pipeline—nearly half of women and a quarter of men report imposter symptoms. Those symptoms strongly predict burnout indices. In other words, our future leaders are being trained in environments that reward polished performance over authentic growth, and they're burning out before they graduate.

The same patterns show up outside healthcare. A widely cited survey by *Blind* (an anonymous professional network) found that 58% of tech employees at companies such as Google, Amazon, and Facebook reported imposter syndrome symptoms. These are some of the most highly recruited, highly paid professionals on the planet—and still they doubt whether they belong.

Three headlines emerge:

1. Prevalence is high in pressure-heavy fields
2. Well-being takes a hit—burnout, anxiety, depression, suicidal ideation
3. Organizations pay twice—once in lost performance now, again in lost leaders later

The bill is coming due, and it doesn't wait for a convenient quarter.

What Happens Inside the Leader

Imposter feelings don't just hurt—they rewire behavior. Leaders driven by fear of exposure fall into predictable loops:

- Overprepare or procrastinate (then cram)
- Avoid risk and decline stretch assignments
- Hoard decisions and under-delegate
- Discount wins as "luck" or "timing"

There's neuroscience behind it.

Researchers studying attribution style found imposter-prone people explain success as *external, unstable, and specific* —"That client liked me," "The market was hot." **This prevents the nervous system from encoding success as**

repeatable. The brain literally doesn't learn: *I can do this again.* Wins slip through the cracks.

Perfectionism adds more fuel. A meta-analysis of 43 studies linked multidimensional perfectionism to higher burnout across education, athletics, and work. Perfectionism provides a fragile power source: it drives sprints but blocks recovery, curiosity, and creativity. Leaders end up working harder and harder for smaller and smaller gains.

The result: you shift from scanning for opportunities to scanning for threats. You speak less, ask fewer questions, and play not to lose. The mask buys you temporary safety, but at the price of long-term smallness.

A corporate story: When Howard Schultz returned as CEO of Starbucks in 2008, the company was in decline. Many executives had been performing certainty—glossy presentations, confident forecasts—but behind the curtain, same-store sales were cratering. Schultz's first act was symbolic humility: shutting down every store for three hours to retrain baristas on making espresso. Wall Street mocked the move. Employees, however, reported relief: "Finally, we're admitting what's broken." That act cracked the mask and restored learning. Within two years, Starbucks returned to growth.

What Happens to the Team

Armored leaders often look effective from the outside: they run tight meetings, make quick calls, and appear decisive. But decisiveness is not the key variable in long-term performance. Learning velocity is.

The Humility Advantage

Amy Edmondson's landmark research on psychological safety showed that teams with higher safety reported *more* errors, not fewer, because people spoke up. Errors surfaced faster, teams learned, and outcomes improved. Silent teams looked clean but broke under stress.

Now connect the dots. When leaders wear a mask, they punish uncertainty—both their own and their team's. People learn to read the weather of the leader's mood instead of the work. Half-formed ideas stay hidden. Risks stay underground. Dashboards stay green while reality turns red.

The damage extends to succession planning. Studies in the *Journal of Vocational Behavior* show that imposter feelings correlate with lower motivation to lead and weaker career planning. Translation: if your culture normalizes masks, you aren't just weakening today's performance—you're starving tomorrow's leadership bench.

A military story: In the U.S. Army, after-action reviews (AARs) are a ritual after every mission. The most senior officer begins by admitting personal mistakes: "Here's what I got wrong." That signal cracks the mask, giving permission for others to surface errors and lessons. Units that rigorously practice AARs learn faster, adapt better, and suffer fewer repeated failures. Compare that to organizations where leaders never admit mistakes: lessons are buried, errors repeat, and morale erodes.

A Story from the Wards

A qualitative study of internal-medicine residents described a haunting cycle:

"I'm terrified of being exposed." → "I don't speak up." → "I overwork to compensate." → "I feel more fraudulent because I'm exhausted." → repeat.

Many linked silence during patient rounds to the fear of public correction. Supervisors who normalized uncertainty created a sense of relief and higher participation. Supervisors who performed invulnerability created fear and silence.

Different industry, same nervous system. Leaders everywhere face the same choice: signal theater (certainty, flawless answers, rapid monologues) or signal learning (clear stakes, known unknowns, time to think, permission to try). One compound's fear. One compound's capability.

The Equity Angle

Imposter experiences don't happen in a vacuum. They interact with identity and context.

Research with racially and ethnically minoritized professionals shows that minority-status stress plus imposter feelings predicts worse mental health. Systems that send "you don't belong" signals make imposter thoughts rational, not irrational.

A 2020 *Journal of Counseling Psychology* study showed that women of color in STEM reported significantly higher imposter scores than their white peers, with the imposter effect compounding discrimination stress. For leaders, the implication is clear: this is not about "fixing" people—it's about redesigning climates.

That's why leaders can't reduce this to "confidence coaching." Individual growth matters, but system design matters just as much. Equal airtime. Public sponsorship. Visible correction of interruptions and credit theft. Ignore the environment, and you'll keep paying the price of churn, caution, and quiet.

The Math of Under-Voice

On paper, risk aversion looks prudent. In practice, it's deadly.

- Every unasked question delays the truth
- Every unspoken doubt extends a bad path
- Every concealed error robs the team of pattern recognition

Edmondson showed that error-suppression cultures collapse suddenly. They look clean—until they don't.

Case example: The Challenger disaster in 1986 wasn't a failure of rocket science; it was a failure of voice. Engineers at Morton Thiokol had flagged concerns about O-ring performance in cold weather. But under pressure from NASA executives performing certainty, dissent was softened, data minimized, and risks downplayed. The result: a tragedy that killed seven astronauts. The mask—"we can't afford to delay, we must project confidence"—costs lives.

Imposter-driven perfectionism makes this worse. Teams built on socially prescribed perfectionism may deliver tidy outputs at first, but they run down energy, creativity, and courage until the system breaks.

What It Feels Like Inside

You'll recognize the mask by these tells:

- You prepare not to serve the decision but to avoid questions
- You delay delegation because visibility scares you
- You leave meetings relieved you "got through it" rather than energized
- Positive feedback bounces off. You credit timing or luck

The mask feels like armor, but it's really a leash.

What Works: Evidence-Backed Moves

You don't remove the mask with platitudes. You replace its fuel.

1. Treat perfectionism.

CBT protocols show that training leaders to set good-enough standards, test catastrophic predictions, and avoid cram cycles reduces imposter symptoms.

2. Practice self-compassion.

A 2023 Randomized Controlled Trial (RCT) showed that even short self-compassion practices lowered imposter scores and perfectionism. Mechanism: reduced self-attack → faster curiosity recovery.

3. Engineer voice.

Don't hope people speak. Design it: "What's one reason this fails?" Call on junior voices first. Credit dissent publicly.

4. Coach attribution.

When wins happen, anchor them in internal, stable, global causes. "We shipped on time because you anticipated the risk." This rewires the "it was luck" reflex.

5. Fix the system.

For underrepresented groups, imposter stress is situational, not personal. Leaders must redesign airtime, credit, and sponsorship.

6. Measure humility.

Stop treating clean dashboards as proof. Track escalations raised, assumptions tested, and reversals made. Learning metrics matter more than optics.

Story: When the Mask Cracks

In general surgery, imposter concerns are rampant. Residents stay silent. Attendings delay presentations until "perfect." Teams quietly default to solo heroics.

One chair tried something radical: "case-confusion rounds." A weekly forum to surface uncertainties, mistakes, and would-do-differently moments. The outcome? More near-misses reported. More cross-service consults are called early. Fewer last-minute crises.

The literature predicted this: imposter stress drives silence and solo overwork. Safety pulls people into shared learning.

Objection Handling

"If I admit uncertainty, I'll lose authority."

The opposite. High-reliability teams trust leaders who say, "Here's what we know, what we don't, and what we'll test." That reads as competence.

"This is just a confidence issue."

Wrong. Mayo Clinic data tied impostorism to burnout and suicidal ideation. It's operational risk.

"It's a woman's problem."

False. Prevalence is high across genders. If you lead, if you're sure you're not an imposter, you're leading imposter-prone people.

"Shouldn't people just toughen up?"

No. Perfectionism breeds fatigue, cynicism, and silence. Tough leaders make truth cheap to say.

A 10-Minute Weekly Practice

Run this ritual for eight weeks.

1. **Two-minute state check.** Breath, long exhale, shoulders down. Intent: "learn fast."
2. **Map unknowns.** "Here are the top three uncertainties."

3. **Invite challenges.** "What am I missing?" Call on low-status voices first.
4. **Surface near-miss.** Rotate who shares one caught-late risk.
5. **Credit candor.** Record what we'll test. Publicly thank the person who improved the plan.

By week 6, speed improves. By week 8, morale rises. The mask loses oxygen.

Leader's Playbook: Spotting the Hidden Costs

Health red flags: Chronic exhaustion, stress-related illness, withdrawal

Behavioral red flags: Silence in meetings, avoidance of stretch work, over-control

Team red flags: Green dashboards hiding red reality, high turnover in juniors, low error reporting

When you see these, you're not looking at individual weakness—you're looking at systemic mask costs.

Reflection Prompt #2

Where are you still trying to *earn* your right to be here?

Name the specific behavior, not the feeling. Then write one sentence you'll say in your next meeting to crack the mask:

"Here's the part of this plan I'm least sure about. Who sees a blind spot I don't?"

Chapter Takeaway

The mask you wear to protect yourself is the same mask that's suffocating your team's potential. Every moment spent defending your image is a moment stolen from serving the mission.

The cost isn't abstract: it shows up in burnout statistics, turnover reports, and innovation metrics. It shows up in the voice that goes unspoken, the error that goes unreported, the successor who never steps forward.

You cannot scale leadership beyond the weight of the armor you carry.

The question isn't whether you'll crack the mask. The question is whether you'll do it intentionally—on your terms, in service of something greater—or whether pressure will crack it for you at the worst possible moment.

Choose the fracture. Initiate the break. Let the gold shine through.

Bridge to Chapter 3

Chapter 2 was the diagnosis—the cost model of the mask. Chapter 3 takes us deeper into the psychological trap many leaders fall into: **The False Self—When Modesty Is Just Self-Doubt in Disguise**. We'll explore how the version of humility that looks virtuous on the surface can actually be fear masquerading as virtue, and how to tell the difference between true humility and its counterfeit twin.

Chapter 3
The False Self—When Modesty Is Just Self-Doubt in Disguise
The most dangerous lies are the ones we mistake for virtue.

In the first two chapters, we explored the cost of the mask: how armor builds a polished exterior while silently taxing health, trust, and innovation. But not all masks look like bravado. Some wear the opposite disguise: a quiet modesty that feels virtuous on the surface but hides something far more corrosive beneath.

This is the "false self" of leadership—the version of you that looks humble but is actually fueled by self-doubt, fear of exposure, or an overlearned reflex to minimize your worth.

Where bravado tries to impress, false modesty tries to disappear. Where armor shouts, the false self whispers: *"Don't notice me too much. Don't expect too much. Don't see how unsure I am."*

It's a different costume, but the same play: self-protection over contribution.

The Psychology of Self-Erasure

Psychologists have long studied the impulse to self-erase—to downplay accomplishments, minimize visibility, or defer excessively to others. On the surface, it looks like humility. In practice, it's a strategy rooted in fear: fear of exposure, fear of rejection, fear that if people look too closely, they'll discover you don't deserve to be here.

The mechanism is familiar to anyone who has battled imposter thoughts:

- A success happens
- Instead of integrating it ("I earned this"), you dismiss it as luck, timing, or someone else's help.
- To avoid future scrutiny, you shrink your presence, defer praise, or preemptively lower expectations.

At first, this can even feel like a strength—who doesn't want a leader who isn't arrogant? But over time, the self-erasure corrodes three things that leadership cannot function without:

1. **Credibility.** Teams don't trust leaders who consistently dodge recognition or refuse ownership of their competence. It reads as false, even if unintentional.
2. **Clarity.** Over-minimizing creates confusion: are you competent or not? The team spends energy trying to guess instead of following.
3. **Contribution.** When you step back to avoid exposure, you withhold ideas, voice, and energy that the team needs.

The result is leadership dissonance: the outward show of humility masking an inward swirl of doubt.

False Humility vs. True Humility

It's worth drawing the line clearly.

True humility is grounded in reality. It acknowledges both strengths and limits with balance. It says, *"I have gifts, and I have gaps. Both can serve the mission."*

False humility is grounded in fear. It refuses to own its strengths and exaggerates its flaws. It says, *"If I minimize myself enough, no one will notice the cracks."*

The difference is posture. One is expansive; the other is shrinking.

A striking example comes from a 2018 study in the *Journal of Applied Psychology* that examined "humblebragging" in workplace contexts. Participants who disguised self-promotion as modesty ("I can't believe I got promoted again; I don't deserve it") were rated as less likable and less competent than those who either owned their strengths openly or showed genuine humility. People can sense the difference between grounded humility and fear-driven false modesty.

Neuroscience: The Cost of the Split Identity

Neuroscience provides another lens. In 2014, Moran and colleagues published research on self-discrepancy—the gap between how we see ourselves and how we think others see us. That gap isn't just psychological; it's biological.

When people experience a mismatch between their actual self and their perceived self, brain regions involved in error monitoring and threat detection light up. In other words, the brain treats identity dissonance like danger. Stress hormones rise, cognitive bandwidth shrinks, and executive functions—planning, decision-making, emotional regulation—get impaired.

That means the "false self" isn't neutral. It actively narrows your leadership capacity. Every time you minimize your voice or disown your strengths, your nervous system interprets it as a threat, pulling energy away from creativity and presence and into protection.

This is why leaders who seem calm in private suddenly freeze or falter in public. It's not a lack of skill—it's a nervous system hijack triggered by the stress of dissonance.

Historical and Philosophical Insights

The tension between reputation and character has been wrestled with for centuries.

The Stoics warned against obsession with appearances. Epictetus said, *"If you want to improve, be content to be thought foolish and stupid."* Marcus Aurelius wrote, *"Don't waste the rest of your time here worrying about other people... It will keep you from doing anything useful."*

Or consider this line often attributed to Epictetus: *"Don't spend time worrying about your reputation—be concerned with your character."*

The Stoics weren't advocating arrogance. They were pointing to the futility of managing an image at the expense of reality. In leadership terms: the more you contort yourself to look modest or invulnerable, the less energy you have to actually build character and competence.

Real-World Stories of the False Self

1. Healthcare: The Junior Surgeon Who Wouldn't Speak Up

A case study published in *BMJ Quality & Safety* described a surgical trainee who noticed a break in sterile protocol but didn't raise it. Later asked why, she admitted: *"I didn't want to look like I was trying to show off or correct my superior."* What looked like modesty was actually fear of exposure. The result? A preventable post-operative infection.

2. Corporate: Satya Nadella's "Learn-It-All" Culture

When Satya Nadella became CEO of Microsoft, he inherited a culture where many employees underplayed ideas out of fear of being wrong in front of "know-it-all" colleagues. Nadella shifted the posture by modeling vulnerability—owning what he didn't know, crediting others' expertise. The result wasn't self-erasure but an empowered voice. Microsoft's turnaround is widely credited to this cultural reset.

3. Military: After-Action Reviews

In the U.S. Army, after-action reviews (AARs) foster open, professional discussions focused on what happened, why it happened, and how to improve future performance. Leaders are encouraged to model accountability by candidly acknowledging both their own and the unit's mistakes, which strengthens credibility and builds trust within the team. Genuine humility—

recognizing shortfalls and accepting responsibility—helps everyone learn and develop, while false modesty or avoidance of responsibility, such as a junior officer downplaying their role, can undermine confidence and hinder professional growth. The goal of AARs is for all ranks to participate honestly, ensuring continual improvement and unit cohesion.

The Organizational Cost of False Modesty

The personal stress of self-doubt would be bad enough. But the cost doesn't stop at the individual.

1. Lost Innovation. When leaders withhold ideas to avoid exposure, organizations lose potential breakthroughs. A 2021 MIT Sloan study found that employees who suppressed their voice due to fear of seeming arrogant contributed 40% fewer process improvements than peers.

2. Team Confusion. Teams read leaders' behavior as data. If you consistently downplay your abilities, people question whether you're competent—or whether they should minimize themselves too.

3. Burnout by Overcompensation. False modesty often pairs with overwork. Leaders try to "prove" themselves silently by doing more behind the scenes, which accelerates exhaustion.

This is why imposter-driven modesty is not a private issue. It's a leadership risk factor.

The Mask Behind the Mask

False humility is tricky because it gets cultural applause.

The Humility Advantage

Many organizations prefer the "safe modest" leader over the "brash arrogant" one. But the danger is that both are masks.

- Arrogance hides insecurity by puffing up.
- False modesty hides insecurity by shrinking down.

Both are self-protection, not service. Both keep attention on the self instead of the mission.

The question isn't whether you look modest. The question is whether you are showing up whole, owning strengths and limits together.

There have been times when I deflected credit. There were three of us on the sales team, and I was the most tenured with the most seasoned relationships. We finished 2nd in the region for the year. I accepted no credit and surrendered all of it to the other two. On the surface, that looks noble, but inside, there was fear. I didn't want to be seen as self-promoting or arrogant, so I hid behind humility. What it really did was rob me—and the team—of a clear example of what leadership and experience could contribute. It blurred accountability and muted the lessons I could have shared. I eventually realized that playing small doesn't inspire anyone; it only makes invisibility comfortable.

Evidence-Based Practices to Close the Gap

So how do you shift from false modesty to authentic humility? Research points to several moves:

1. Self-Compassion Training

Kristin Neff's work shows that self-compassion reduces self-criticism and increases resilience. Leaders who practice self-kindness are less likely to deflect praise or disown success.

A practical example of self-compassion training, based on Kristin Neff's work, is the "Self-Compassion Break" exercise, which is widely used to help individuals respond to their own difficulties with greater kindness and understanding.

Example: Self-Compassion Break

- When facing a stressful moment, pause and acknowledge the difficulty—mentally noting, "This is a tough situation," or "This hurts."

- Remind yourself that suffering and imperfection are part of the shared human experience: say, "Others feel this way too," or "I'm not alone."

- Then, offer yourself kindness and self-support. You might say, "May I be kind to myself," or "May I accept myself as I am."

- To deepen the effect, you can place a hand on your heart or give yourself a gentle hug, which helps self-soothe.

2. Attribution Coaching

Studies by Brauer et al. show that imposter-prone individuals consistently externalize success. Leaders can rewire this by journaling or verbally owning contributions: "This outcome happened because of my preparation and collaboration."

3. Feedback Reframing

Encourage leaders to practice receiving praise without deflection. Instead of "It was nothing," try "Thank you—I worked hard on that." It feels awkward at first, but it builds alignment between external recognition and internal ownership.

4. Contextual Cues

Organizational cues matter. Leaders must explicitly separate humility from erasure by rewarding both *acknowledgment of strengths* and *acknowledgment of limits*.

A Leadership Playbook: Moving from False Self to Real Self

Step 1: Notice the Tell.

Do you dodge credit reflexively? Do you shrink your language ("I just got lucky," "It wasn't me")? That's the false self talking.

Step 2: Own One Strength.

Each week, write down one win and the specific skills you brought to it. Share it with a trusted peer or mentor.

Step 3: Model Balanced Humility.

In meetings, pair strength with uncertainty: "I'm confident in our direction, and here's one area I'll need your help with."

Step 4: Invite Accurate Mirrors.

Ask a direct report or peer: "What strengths do you see in me that I tend to minimize?" Let them reflect on what you can't.

Step 5: Separate Fear from Service.

Before deflecting praise, ask: "Am I shrinking to serve the mission, or to protect myself?"

Reflection Prompt #3

Where do you practice "false humility"—minimizing yourself to avoid exposure rather than to serve truth? Write one sentence you could say in your next meeting that balances strength and openness.

Example: *"I'm confident this approach is sound. The risk I want us to examine is..."*

Chapter Takeaway

The false self is seductive because it looks like virtue. It masquerades as humility, but it is really fear in disguise.

True humility is not shrinking; it is standing whole. It owns strengths without arrogance and weaknesses without shame.

The Stoics had it right: stop worrying about your reputation and build your character. In the end, your team doesn't need you to look humble. They need you to be real—strong enough to own your gifts, grounded enough to admit your limits, and wise enough to know the difference.

That is the leader people trust. That is the leader who uncovers the gold within.

Bridge to Chapter 4

Chapter 3 revealed the trap of the false self—how modesty rooted in fear erodes credibility, confuses teams, and keeps leaders from showing up whole. The danger isn't just arrogance at the top of the spectrum or self-erasure at the other end—it's the oscillation between the two, the exhausting swing between overcompensating and hiding.

But where does this voice come from? Why does the false self feel so convincing, so persistent, so hard to silence?

Chapter 4 takes us to the source: **Unmasking the Inner Critic**—the invisible saboteur that keeps leaders playing small, chasing perfection, or drowning in overwork. If the false self is how we present ourselves outwardly, the inner critic is the running commentary inwardly. And until we learn to disarm it, we'll keep performing instead of leading.

Let's go find where that voice began—and how to silence it for good.

Chapter 4
Unmasking the Inner Critic
The most dangerous voice in leadership is rarely the loudest one in the room. It's the quiet one in your own head.

This quiet voice—your inner critic—has derailed more promising leaders than any external challenge ever could.

This is the inner critic: the invisible saboteur that keeps leaders playing small, chasing perfection, or drowning in overwork. If the false self (Chapter 3) is how we present ourselves outwardly, the inner critic is the running commentary inwardly—the voice that shapes whether we step forward, hesitate, or retreat.

Every leader carries this voice to some degree. The question is not whether it exists, but whether it drives.

The Roots of the Inner Critic

Psychologists trace the inner critic to early socialization. As children, we learn which behaviors bring acceptance and which trigger rejection. Over time, external criticism gets internalized into self-talk. A parent's "Don't mess this up," a teacher's "You can do better," or a coach's "Mistakes are unacceptable" can all evolve into inner scripts that echo decades later, even though oftentimes the messenger was well-meaning.

I remember years ago – I couldn't have been older than 5 years – waiting on the front porch of our apartment complex for my Dad, who was running errands and was supposed to bring me a baseball glove. I was so excited when he pulled up. As he walked up to the steps upon which I was sitting, he said, "I forgot your glove," and walked into the apartment. I sobbed. He then walked back out and handed me the baseball glove and said, "I don't know what you're crying about." He didn't mean to shame me—but the message landed anyway: *Your feelings are inappropriate. Manage better.* That voice became part of my inner critic's greatest hits collection.

Perfectionist tendencies amplify the critic. Studies in the *Journal of Personality and Social Psychology* show that perfectionism—especially "socially prescribed perfectionism" (believing others demand flawlessness)—is strongly linked with harsh self-talk and chronic self-doubt. Leaders caught in this loop may appear driven on the outside, but their motivation is fueled by fear of failure rather than pursuit of excellence.

Meta-analytic work finds that perfectionistic concerns (self-criticism, fear of mistakes) are moderately to strongly related to burnout, far more than healthy striving. This helps explain why high achievers with a harsh inner voice tend toward exhaustion rather than growth.

A all-too-common story: A senior executive once described it this way: "Every time I present to the board, it's like I bring my sixth-grade teacher with me. She's right there, waiting to mark me down." Decades of achievements hadn't silenced the voice; they had only raised the stakes. This is strikingly similar to me hearing my dad's voice, "I don't know what you're crying about!"

Neuroscience: Why the Critic Feels So Real

The inner critic isn't just a psychological construct—it's a neurological pattern etched into the brain's survival systems. What feels like a "voice" of doubt is actually a series of circuits firing in predictable ways, shaped by evolution and reinforced by habit.

Default Mode Network (DMN): The Rumination Engine

At the core of the inner critic lies the Default Mode Network, a set of brain hubs that light up whenever we're thinking about ourselves. On one hand, the DMN allows for reflection and self-awareness—valuable skills for growth. But when hijacked by self-judgment, it fuels rumination: the endless "what if I fail," "I'm not good enough," or "they'll see through me" loops, or "I don't know what you're crying about."

Neuroscience research consistently shows that hyperactivity in the DMN is linked to anxiety and depression. Leaders stuck in this loop not only feel emotionally drained but also find it harder to make clear, forward-looking decisions.

Encouragingly, studies demonstrate that mindfulness-based interventions quiet DMN overactivity. The effect on rumination isn't massive, but it's real and consistent. In other words, this circuitry is trainable—<u>you can rewire the critic.</u>

Cortisol & the Stress Cascade

Self-criticism doesn't stay in the mind; it floods the body. Harsh inner dialogue triggers the hypothalamic-pituitary-adrenal (HPA) axis, spiking cortisol. Elevated cortisol narrows cognitive bandwidth, weakens working memory, and impairs executive functions such as problem-solving and emotional regulation—the very abilities leaders depend on in high-stakes moments.

Picture a hospital administrator in a crisis: if their inner critic whispers "you're blowing it," the resulting stress response makes it harder to access calm, creative solutions. What feels like a private mental battle is actually a full-body stress event.

Self-Discrepancy & the Brain's Error Alarms

When there is a gap between your actual self and your idealized self, brain regions such as the anterior cingulate cortex (ACC) and the medial prefrontal cortex (mPFC) become active. Biologically, this activation signals an "identity mismatch," meaning the brain recognizes a discrepancy in self-perception as a problem requiring resolution.

Anterior Cingulate Cortex (ACC) and Identity Mismatch

The ACC is involved in high-level functions like attention allocation, error detection, decision-making, and emotional processing. It plays a critical role in responding to self-conscious emotions, which arise when one's actions or traits fall short of social or personal standards. This region coordinates emotional and physiological responses, effectively flagging situations that involve conflict or error—such as the mismatch between actual and ideal selves—and signaling the need for adjustment or correction. [pmc.ncbi.nlm.nih +1]

Medial Prefrontal Cortex (mPFC) and Self-Reference

The medial prefrontal cortex is heavily implicated in self-referential thinking, including reflecting on one's identity, goals, and personal values. Activation in the mPFC during identity mismatch reflects the brain's attempt to process and reconcile differences between the current state and an idealized version of the self. This monitoring and evaluative function helps guide behavior toward reducing the disparity. [pmc.ncbi.nlm.nih]

Biological Basis of Identity Mismatch as a "Problem"

The brain treats the gap between actual and ideal self as a salient error or conflict requiring immediate attention. The ACC's role in performance monitoring and error signaling extends into social and emotional domains, where it coordinates neural and physiological responses to motivate behavior change. The mPFC contributes by updating self-related information and maintaining a dynamic sense of self-concept, which is crucial for adaptive functioning. [wikipedia +1]

In summary, the anterior cingulate cortex signals the emotional and cognitive conflict in identity mismatch, while the medial prefrontal cortex handles self-referential processing to help resolve the discrepancy. Together, these regions help the brain treat the difference between actual and ideal self as a problem demanding correction, driving efforts toward self-improvement or adjustment in perceptions.

This dynamic reflects how deeply intertwined our brain's emotional, cognitive, and social functions are in maintaining a coherent and adaptive sense of identity.

That's why the critic's voice feels so urgent and convincing: your brain is literally sounding an alarm, pushing you to close the gap, even if the "problem" is based on distorted thinking rather than truth.

Leadership Implications: Why False Feels True

In leadership terms, every time you minimize your contribution, disown your strengths, or catastrophize a mistake, you aren't just "thinking negatively." You're activating stress physiology, narrowing your leadership capacity, and wiring your brain to perceive threat where none exists.

The critic feels real because it uses the same biological systems designed to keep us alive in emergencies. Unfortunately, in modern leadership, that wiring often backfires. Instead of sharpening focus, it blinds perspective. Instead of fueling growth, it locks us in survival mode.

Here's the critical insight: the mPFC isn't malfunctioning—it's working with corrupted data. It's trying to close the gap between who you are and who you *think* you should be. But that 'should' is built from clay layers, not gold. The practices that follow don't silence the brain's error detection—they recalibrate it. When you chip away the false ideal (the perfect leader who never doubts), your brain can finally recognize the real ideal: the leader you already are beneath the armor.

The takeaway is simple but profound: if you've ever felt like an imposter, it's not proof you're failing—it's proof your brain is running a pattern. The voice of the critic is urgent, but it is not accurate. And because these circuits are trainable, leaders can learn to step out of the critic's grip and return to calm, creative command.

The Critic's Favorite Weapons: Thought Distortions

The inner critic rarely attacks head-on. Instead, it works like a skilled illusionist, bending perception until the distortion feels like reality. In cognitive-behavioral therapy (CBT), these mental traps are called *cognitive distortions*—systematic errors in thinking that cloud judgment and intensify self-doubt.

For leaders, they are especially dangerous because they don't just affect self-esteem—they directly shape decisions, communication, and organizational culture.

1. All-or-Nothing Thinking: Perfection or Failure

"If I don't nail this presentation, I'm a failure."

This distortion leaves no room for nuance. A strong performance is never "good enough" unless it's flawless, and a single stumble becomes a total collapse. Neuroscience shows that this black-and-white thinking is linked to heightened amygdala activity, the brain's threat detector, which interprets even small mistakes as existential dangers.

In leadership, this can cause paralysis—leaders avoid taking on bold initiatives unless they're sure of perfection, robbing their teams of creativity and momentum.

2. Discounting the Positive: Success Doesn't Count

"Sure, the meeting went well, but it was just luck."

The critic is notorious for moving the goalposts. No matter how many wins you achieve, it reinterprets them as flukes or external accidents. This undermines the dopamine reward cycle in the brain—normally, success releases dopamine that reinforces motivation. But when the critic discounts achievements, that reinforcement is blocked. Leaders stuck here often burn out because they're expending energy without ever internalizing satisfaction.

3. Catastrophizing: Imagining the Worst

"If this project stumbles, my career is over."

Catastrophizing exaggerates risk and consequence, magnifying a molehill into a mountain. This distortion activates the body's stress response—cortisol spikes, heart rate rises, and the brain shifts into fight-or-flight mode. The result is tunnel vision: instead of weighing options calmly, leaders default to survival strategies like avoidance, micromanagement, or overreactions.

4. Mind Reading: Assuming the Worst About Others' Thoughts

"They probably think I don't know what I'm talking about."

The critic convinces leaders they have access to others' unspoken judgments. But in reality, mind reading is projection—our own doubts reflected back onto others. fMRI studies show that when people attempt to infer others' thoughts, the same brain regions involved in self-evaluation—particularly the medial prefrontal cortex (mPFC) and temporoparietal junction (TPJ)—light up, which means we often confuse our own insecurities with others' perceptions.

The leadership cost? Leaders hesitate to voice ideas or push back, leaving influence and innovation on the table.

5. Overgeneralization: One Mistake Becomes an Identity

"I stumbled once, so I'll always stumble."

Overgeneralization is when the brain's pattern-recognition system runs wild, mistaking isolated setbacks for permanent truth. A failed pitch becomes evidence that you're "bad at presenting." A difficult conversation gone wrong becomes proof you're "terrible with people."

Over time, these distortions sculpt identity itself, embedding false limitations into how leaders see themselves and what risks they're willing to take.

Why Leaders Believe the Critic

Why does such an obviously negative voice hold so much power? If a colleague spoke to us the way our inner critic does, we'd probably dismiss them—or at least challenge their credibility. Yet when the voice comes from within, leaders often grant it unearned authority.

1. It Pretends to Protect

The critic often frames itself as helpful: *"If I scare you enough, you won't make a mistake."* In evolutionary terms, the brain is wired to anticipate danger and prevent failure—better to err on the side of caution than to miss a potential threat. The critic hijacks this bias, convincing leaders that harsh self-talk is a form of vigilance.

"Don't blow this presentation," it says, as if anxiety itself were a strategy for success. In reality, the stress response narrows creativity and increases error rates. What feels like protection is actually sabotage.

2. It Draws Authority from the Past

The critic's voice rarely emerges in a vacuum. Its tone often echoes parents, teachers, coaches, or early bosses who used criticism as motivation. Because those authority figures shaped our formative experiences, their voices became internalized.

Neuroscience research shows that the brain uses stored social memories—especially of authority figures—as templates for current evaluation. That's why a leader in their 50s can still hear a high-school teacher's tone when they make a mistake. Even if the content is outdated, the emotional weight remains, and the critic borrows that weight to sound credible.

3. It Exploits Uncertainty

Leadership thrives in ambiguity. Markets shift, regulations change, teams evolve, and outcomes are rarely predictable. Yet the brain dislikes silence and uncertainty; it seeks patterns and explanations. The critic rushes in to fill that gap: *"If you don't know what will happen, it must be because you're not capable."*

Instead of tolerating uncertainty as part of the leadership landscape, leaders mistake the critic's commentary for useful analysis. This not only drains confidence but also leads to hesitation and missed opportunities.

Disarming the Inner Critic Through Awareness

The paradox of the inner critic is that the harder you try to silence it, the louder it often becomes. Leaders who attempt to "battle" the critic with willpower discover that resistance only reinforces its authority. The way forward isn't suppression—it's awareness.

Psychologists call this *cognitive defusion*: learning to separate yourself from your thoughts instead of being fused to them. Once you realize, *"I am not my thoughts; I am the observer of my thoughts,"* the critic begins to lose its grip.

Practical Moves for Creating Distance from the Inner Critic:

1. Name the Voice

Give your critic a persona—"The Judge," "The Drill Sergeant," "The Doubter." I named mine "Satan." Ironically, after my wife went through my coaching program, she named her inner critic "Satan" as well. This simple act externalizes the voice, transforming it from an all-powerful "truth" into a character you can engage with more playfully. Leaders often find that once the critic has a name, it loses much of its intimidation power.

2. Notice the Pattern

Track the critic's lines for a week. Write down the exact phrases it uses—"You're not ready," "They'll see through you," "Don't mess this up." Very quickly, you'll realize your critic doesn't have new material; it's recycling the same script on a loop. Recognizing this predictability reframes the critic as a broken record rather than a credible advisor.

3. Shift from Identification to Observation

Language matters. Instead of saying, *"I'm failing,"* experiment with, *"I'm having the thought that I'm failing."* This micro-shift creates psychological distance. It reminds the brain that thoughts are events—not facts. Leaders who use this move report that emotions feel less overwhelming, and performance anxiety loses its sting.

The Mindfulness Advantage

Awareness practices are amplified by mindfulness, which trains attention to notice thoughts without judgment. Meta-analyses of mindfulness-based programs show reliable reductions in rumination and improvements in emotion regulation.

For leaders, this isn't abstract—it's a physiological counterweight. Mindfulness literally downregulates the stress response, calming the critic's surge and restoring access to the prefrontal cortex—the seat of judgment, planning, and executive control.

The Humility Advantage

Two Research-Backed Techniques Leaders Can Use to Quiet the Critic in the Moment:

1. Affect Labeling

When the critic stirs up anxiety, put the emotion into words: *"I'm noticing anxiety and embarrassment."* Neuroscientific studies from UCLA and others show that naming feelings reduces amygdala activation (the brain's alarm system) and increases prefrontal control.

In leadership terms, this means you can literally turn the emotional "volume" down during a board presentation, difficult feedback conversation, or crisis briefing—regaining clarity when it matters most.

2. Distanced Self-Talk

Address yourself by name (*"Alex, focus on the first slide"*) or in the second person (*"You've done this before—just start"*). This small linguistic tweak creates psychological distance, similar to how you'd encourage a colleague.

Research shows that distanced self-talk measurably improves emotion regulation and performance under pressure. Leaders who practice this consistently often describe it as "coaching themselves from the outside," transforming the critic's voice into one of support rather than sabotage.

The 3-Step Reset: A Practice You Can Use Today

Here's a simple sequence to disarm the critic in real-time:

Step 1: Catch it.

Notice when the critic speaks. "There it is—the voice saying I'm not ready."

Step 2: Name the distortion.

"That's catastrophizing. One misstep doesn't end my career."

Step 3: Replace with grounded truth.

"I've led through uncertainty before. I can handle what comes next."

This takes 30 seconds. Practice it before your next high-stakes moment. Over time, the critic's voice weakens, and your own steady leadership voice strengthens.

Real-World Story: When the Critic Gets Louder

A hospital CEO admitted in coaching: "Every board meeting, my inner critic says, 'You're just a doctor pretending to be an executive.'" She'd risen through clinical excellence but constantly felt like an imposter in the C-suite.

She mapped her critic's favorite distortions: discounting wins ("The hospital's turnaround was the team, not me"), catastrophizing ("One bad quarter and I'm done"), and mind-reading ("The board thinks I'm out of my depth").

Then she practiced the three-step reset before each meeting. Within three months, she reported, "The voice is still there, but it doesn't drive anymore. Most of that clay is peeled away. I can hear it—and choose to lead anyway."

That's the goal. Not silencing the critic forever—that's unrealistic—but shrinking its influence until it becomes background noise rather than a hijacker of decisions.

Reflection Prompt #4

Think of a recent moment when your inner critic spoke the loudest. Write down the exact words it used. Now, label the distortion (all-or-nothing, catastrophizing, etc.) and replace it with one grounded truth you can carry forward.

Chapter Takeaway

The inner critic will never vanish entirely—it's part of being human. But it doesn't have to drive.

The work of leadership is not silencing every negative thought; it's recognizing them for what they are: echoes of the past, not prophecies of the future. When you shift from identification to observation, from distortion to grounded truth, you transform the critic from saboteur into signal—an invitation to re-center.

You've now completed the foundation. You understand what imposter syndrome is (Chapter 1), what it costs (Chapter 2), how false humility disguises it (Chapter 3), and where the inner critic comes from (Chapter 4).

Now comes the transformation

Part II begins with the question every leader who's read this far is asking: *"Okay, I see the problem at every level. Now, how do I actually fix it?"*

The answer starts in Chapter 5, where we'll rewire humility from the inside out—not as weakness, but as the neurological and relational superpower it truly is.

Let's begin the rebuild.

Assess your leadership style - Free

Part II: Reclaiming Your Power

Chapter 5
Humility Rewired—Building Strength from the Inside Out

Humility is often misunderstood as weakness. In truth, it is one of the most neurologically and relationally powerful states a leader can cultivate.

Where the inner critic constricts, humility expands. Where self-doubt narrows perspective, humility opens new channels of empathy, trust, and long-term thinking.

Modern neuroscience shows that humility is not simply a moral virtue; it is a measurable brain state. It activates the neural circuitry for empathy, cooperation, and foresight. Hormonal research demonstrates that it releases biochemical trust signals that make teams cohere. And leadership studies across healthcare, aviation, and technology confirm that humble leaders outperform arrogant or self-focused peers—not by projecting dominance, but by expanding collective capacity.

Humility is strength rewired, built from the inside out.

The Neuroscience of Humility

Humility engages key brain regions that support high-level leadership functions:

1. Prefrontal Cortex (PFC)

The PFC governs executive functions like planning, inhibition, and long-term thinking. Research in Social

Cognitive and Affective Neuroscience found humility correlates with greater activity in the dorsolateral PFC—suggesting humble reflection enhances foresight and reduces impulsive, ego-driven reactions.

2. Anterior Cingulate Cortex (ACC)

Associated with error detection and conflict monitoring, the ACC lights up when we notice gaps between intention and behavior. Humble leaders use this signal not as shame, but as learning.

Here's an example: When a leader plans to stay calm but reacts defensively instead, the anterior cingulate cortex (ACC) lights up—it's the brain's built-in error detector noticing the gap between intention and behavior. Rather than feeling shame, a humble leader sees this as feedback: "That's not how I meant to show up." They pause, reflect, and adjust next time. In other words, humility turns the brain's "you messed up" signal into a learning opportunity.

3. Mirror Neuron System

These neural circuits fire when we observe another's behavior or emotion, underpinning empathy. Humility heightens mirror neuron sensitivity by reducing self-focus, allowing leaders to tune more deeply into others' states. When you see someone cry—whether it's a real person or a movie character—your mirror neuron system activates. These are the brain cells that "mirror" what you observe, helping you feel what others feel. If you're naturally sensitive and empathetic, your mirror neurons fire even more strongly, almost letting you borrow someone else's emotion for a moment.

4. Default Mode Network (DMN)

Overactivation of the DMN fuels rumination and ego-preoccupation. Humility reduces DMN noise, freeing up cognitive bandwidth for present-centered listening and strategic thought.

Case example: A 2018 fMRI study by Rowatt et al. demonstrated that individuals high in trait humility showed greater activation in brain regions linked with perspective-taking and prosocial reasoning when evaluating moral dilemmas. In practical terms, humility literally primes the brain for ethical, people-centered decision-making.

Nervous system note: Leaders who train humility-adjacent skills (mindful awareness, perspective-taking) often show higher heart rate variability (HRV)—a marker of vagal tone associated with emotion regulation and flexible responding. In the moment that would trigger a defensive snap, higher HRV buys you milliseconds of choice. Those milliseconds are where humble leadership lives.

Hormones of Trust: The Biology of Connection

Humility is not just cognitive; it is chemical.

Oxytocin: The "Bonding Hormone"

Paul Zak's work demonstrated oxytocin surges in contexts of empathy and vulnerability, reinforcing generosity and trust. When leaders model humility—by admitting uncertainty, crediting others, or showing vulnerability—oxytocin rises, strengthening team cohesion.

Cortisol Reduction

Humble leaders create psychological safety. When subordinates feel safe, cortisol drops. Lower cortisol levels mean higher creativity, memory recall, and problem-solving ability.

Serotonin Stability

Healthy humility stabilizes serotonin, which regulates mood and social confidence. Dominance-driven hierarchies destabilize this balance; humble climates normalize it.

Healthcare study: A 2021 BMJ Leader study found that physicians rated as "humble" were significantly more trusted by both colleagues and patients. Trust correlated with oxytocin responses measured indirectly through biomarkers. Translation: humility changes body chemistry at both ends of the relationship.

Caveat worth naming: Oxytocin amplifies in-group trust; without inclusive norms, it can unintentionally heighten "us vs them." Humble leadership counterbalances that by widening the circle—explicitly inviting dissenting voices and out-group perspectives so connection doesn't calcify into a clique.

Humility and Emotional Intelligence: The Missing Link

Emotional intelligence (EI) has four pillars: self-awareness, self-regulation, social awareness, and relationship management. Humility acts as the operating system that makes them possible.

- **Self-Awareness:** Humility allows leaders to acknowledge their strengths and limits without distorting them. Without humility, awareness collapses into defensiveness.
- **Self-Regulation:** Humility dampens reactivity. Instead of protecting ego, leaders regulate the state for service.
- **Social-Awareness:** Humility removes the filter of "How does this make me look?" and replaces it with "What is this person experiencing?"
- **Relationship Management:** Humility transforms influence from control to connection.

A meta-analysis in the Journal of Organizational Behavior (Miao et al., 2018) found that EI predicted leadership effectiveness across industries. Importantly, humility moderated this effect: leaders high in EI but low in humility sometimes weaponized empathy for manipulation. Leaders high in both produced the strongest outcomes.

From Reactivity to Intentional Presence

Most leadership breakdowns happen in milliseconds: a defensive snap, a dismissive interruption, a reactive email. Humility rewires this reflex.

- **Reactivity is ego-protection:** fast, narrow, self-centered.
- **Presence is humility in action:** slow enough to notice, broad enough to include others, centered enough to choose

Neuroscience shows mindfulness training—closely tied to humility—reduces amygdala reactivity and strengthens prefrontal control. A JAMA meta-analysis found mindfulness interventions produced small to moderate reductions in anxiety and reactivity, giving leaders more space to respond with intention.

Aviation example: After the 1977 Tenerife disaster, the airline industry overhauled cockpit culture through Crew Resource Management (CRM). Pilots were trained to replace reactivity ("Captain knows best") with intentional voice ("State your concern, pause, listen"). Today, aviation safety is directly tied to humble communication protocols—leaders regulating ego in favor of presence.

Micro-behaviors that save flights (and meetings): CRM boils down to repeatable moves any team can borrow: say the person's name; state the observation; name the risk; propose an action; call for confirmation. That sequence—Name → Fact → Risk → Proposal → Confirm—displaces deference with clarity. It works at 35,000 feet and in Tuesday's product review.

For business settings, you can adapt the steps slightly to fit: **C-L-E-A-R (reframed acronym) C**all by *Name* → **L**ay out the *Fact* → **E**xpress the *Risk* → **A**dvise an *Action* → **R**equest *Confirmation*.

Leadership Case Studies

Healthcare: Humility in the ICU

The Michigan Keystone ICU Project normalized speaking up through checklists and team voice. Physicians invited nurses to stop procedures if the protocol wasn't followed. The result: infection rates plummeted. Humility by design turned voice into safety.

Technology: Tim Cook's Quiet Leadership

When Tim Cook succeeded Steve Jobs at Apple, analysts worried he lacked Jobs's charisma. Instead, Cook brought a different strength: humility grounded in listening. In his first years as CEO, he met with employees across levels, asked questions rather than issuing pronouncements, and publicly credited teams for successes. In a 2013 interview with Bloomberg Businessweek, Cook said, "My job is to make the best decision I can... not to make the best decision that makes me look good." That distinction—mission over image—has been central to his leadership. Under his tenure, Apple became the first trillion-dollar company, demonstrating that humble leadership can drive extraordinary performance.

Technology: Jensen Huang's Learning Posture

NVIDIA CEO Jensen Huang is known for his phrase "I don't know" in executive meetings—not as a weakness, but as an invitation. In interviews and internal communications, Huang consistently emphasizes that rapid technological change demands constant learning. He's been documented asking engineers to teach him about new architectures, publicly acknowledging when competitors innovate ahead of Nvidia, and reframing setbacks as "learning faster than the competition." This humble learning posture has helped Nvidia dominate the AI chip market, with the company's value surging as it leads the generative AI revolution. Huang's willingness not to know created a culture where truth-telling and rapid iteration became competitive advantages.

J. Alexander

Military: U.S. Marine Corps After-Action Reviews

In the Marine Corps, it is suggested that every mission—whether an operation or a field exercise—ends with an After-Action Review (AAR). The focus is simple: what was supposed to happen, what actually happened, what went well, and what can be improved next time. While not required by formal policy, many respected leaders model humility by taking responsibility first—saying things like, "I misjudged the terrain," or "I should have shifted the squad earlier." This sets the tone for honest feedback and learning without fear of blame. It reflects a core Marine principle: fierce accountability toward the mission, respect, and humility toward teammates. Units that embrace this practice adapt faster, correct errors quicker, and build unshakable trust under pressure.

Corporate: Pixar's Braintrust

Pixar created a culture of critique where directors present films in progress to peers. Feedback is candid, but never personal. Humility is baked into the process: leaders must release ego to let the story improve. Pixar's track record of creative hits is a direct outcome of systematized humble learning.

Tech: Google's SRE Practice

Google popularized the blameless postmortem—a review of outages in which human error is treated as a signal of system design, not a reason to shame. The posture is humble by definition: assume competent people in imperfect systems, then fix the system. That stance keeps curiosity high and fear low, so truths surface fast.

Practical Tools: Rewiring Humility

1. The Pause-and-Presence Drill

Before responding in a high-stakes moment: exhale slowly, ask "What outcome matters most here—my image or the mission?" and only then respond.

2. Gratitude Reframe

When receiving credit, replace deflection ("It was nothing") with shared ownership: "Thank you—I'm proud of what the team accomplished." Or, "Thank you – I worked really hard on that."

3. Perspective Switch

Intentionally imagine what the other person is experiencing in a meeting. This primes mirror neurons for empathy.

4. Oxytocin Builders

Zak's research shows oxytocin rises when people feel trusted. Use eye contact, genuine listening, and personal connection to chemically reinforce trust.

5. Feedback Rituals

Adopt Pixar's Braintrust principle: critique the work, not the person. This keeps humility active while sharpening outcomes.

6. Structured Pauses

Healthcare organizations like Mayo Clinic train leaders to pause for three seconds before responding to difficult input. This delay interrupts reactivity and signals humility.

7. The "Two Admits" Rule

In any contentious discussion, commit to admitting two things you learned or got wrong before defending your view. This creates ACC-aligned learning (error-detection without shame) and disarms defensiveness in the room.

8. The "Ask-Then-Answer" Turn

Before presenting a solution, ask: "What's the core constraint as you see it?" You'll surface hidden data, increase buy-in, and often save yourself from solving the wrong problem.

Historical and Philosophical Anchors

Humility has always been central to enduring leadership.

Stoic Philosophy: Epictetus warned against obsession with reputation: "If you want to improve, be content to be thought foolish and stupid." The Stoics understood humility as clarity—not shrinking, but freedom from image management.

Religious Traditions: Across faiths, humility is linked with service. In the Christian tradition, Christ washing His disciples' feet is a radical act of humble leadership—flipping hierarchy to empower others.

Modern Thought: Jim Collins, in *Good to Great*, identified "Level 5 Leaders" as those combining personal humility with fierce resolve. His research showed these leaders built companies that outperformed peers over decades.

A practical Stoic move: Marcus Aurelius often wrote short reminders to himself before meetings ("You will meet meddling, ungrateful people..."). Translate that to leadership today: write a 30-second pre-brief to self ("Expect pushback; choose curiosity; ask one clarifying question before advocating"). That tiny script shifts you from impression management to intention management.

Risks of Misapplied Humility

Not all "humility" is healthy.

- **False Modesty:** Leaders minimize themselves to avoid exposure
- **Self-Silencing:** Humility turns into withdrawal, depriving teams of needed voice
- **Humility Theater:** Leaders brand themselves as "servant leaders" while secretly hoarding control

Authentic humility is accurate self-awareness in service of the mission. It is neither grandstanding nor erasure.

Diagnostic test: Ask: Does my "humility" increase information flow and shared ownership—or reduce it? If truth and initiative are shrinking, you're in false modesty, not humble leadership.

Leader's Playbook: Building Humility as Capacity

1. Daily Self-Check: At day's end, ask: Where did I react to protect ego instead of serve mission?

2. Trust Audit: Identify who on your team hesitates to speak the truth. What would lower their cortisol and raise their oxytocin?

3. Perspective Practice: In one meeting a week, say: "Here's what I don't know and where I need your input."

4. Learning Loop: Model curiosity by asking one genuine, non-rhetorical question in every conversation.

5. Celebrate Vulnerability: Publicly acknowledge when candor improved a decision. Stories spread safety faster than policies.

6. Cross-Industry Borrowing: Healthcare can learn from aviation checklists; tech can learn from ICU safety culture. Build humility by adopting proven structures outside your field.

7. 30-Day Humility Sprint: For four weeks, rotate these habits:

- Week 1: Two Admits Rule
    - Challenge: Each team member must openly admit two personal mistakes or misjudgments this week.
    - Example: "I overestimated how long that meeting would take, and I didn't communicate the delay soon enough."
- Week 2: Conduct a Blameless Review of a Small Miss
    - Challenge: Pick one small setback and analyze it as a team without blame — focus only on learning.
    - Example: "We missed a follow-up call window; next time, we'll set a shared reminder instead of relying on memory."

- Week 3: Junior-First Speaking Order
  - Challenge: In every meeting, let the most junior person speak first before leadership weighs in.
  - Example: "Before I share my thoughts, I want to hear from the new analyst — what's your take?" You may want to let them know ahead of time so you don't give them a panic attack.
- Week 4: Documented Assumptions Log with Revisit Date
  - Challenge: Write down every key assumption behind your current strategy and set a date to test each one.
  - Example: "Assumption: The hospital will renew the contract next quarter — verify by March 15."
- Debrief: What Changed
  - Challenge: At the end of Week 4, review how these small experiments affected team trust, communication, and decision-making.
  - Example: "Since we started junior-first discussions, quieter team members are speaking up — and our ideas are sharper."

Measurement: How to Know It's Working

Humility is not a vibe; it's observable.

Leading Indicators - predict future performance—they're the behaviors that signal humble leadership before you see results:

- Number of assumptions logged before decisions

- Count of early escalations (raised risks before incidents)
- Voice distribution (how many unique speakers per meeting; junior-first rates)

Lagging Indicators - confirm that change has already occurred—they're the outcomes that prove humble leadership is working:

- Rework reduction after reflection reviews
- Time-to-truth (days from first signal to action)
- Retention of high-potential, historically quiet contributors

Track these for one quarter. If humility is rewiring the team, you'll see earlier signals, more balanced participation, and fewer surprises.

Reflection Prompt #5

Think back to your last moment of reactivity. What triggered it—ego, fear, image protection? Write one sentence reframing how you could have responded with humility.

Example: Instead of "I need to prove I'm right," try "I need to clarify what will serve the mission."

Chapter Takeaway

Humility is not about lowering yourself. It is about grounding yourself—rewiring your brain, your hormones, and your presence to create space for others.

It is empathy wired through mirror neurons.

It is foresight built on prefrontal control.

It is trust released through oxytocin.

It is influence rooted not in dominance but in connection.

When humility is rewired as strength, leaders stop performing and start transforming.

Bridge to Chapter 6

If Chapter 5 showed how humility rewires the brain and body for stronger, more connected leadership, Chapter 6 will take the next step: **From Inner Capacity to Outer Voice**.

You've learned the neuroscience. You've practiced the micro-behaviors. Now it's time to rewrite the internal script that's been running your leadership—the stories you tell yourself about who you are, what you're allowed to say, and what you deserve.

Chapter 6: **Rewriting the Script—Tools to Reclaim Your Voice** will show you how to shift from limiting beliefs to empowering identity, from unconscious scripting to conscious authorship. This is where you stop living someone else's narrative and start writing your own.

The transformation continues.

Chapter 6
Rewriting the Script— Tools to Reclaim Your Voice

Every leader carries a script—an internal narrative about who they are, how much they belong, and what they're allowed to say. The question is: who wrote yours?

For some, the script empowers: "I can learn, adapt, and grow." For others, the script constrains: "Don't speak up or you'll be exposed." Most leaders never question the origin of these narratives. They simply obey them, treating whispers from childhood wounds and early career setbacks as immutable truths about their capabilities.

The trouble is, most of us didn't write the script we're running. It was drafted for us—by childhood voices, early bosses, cultural expectations, or repeated experiences of success and failure. By the time we step into high-stakes leadership, the script feels natural, inevitable. But it is not.

This chapter is about rewriting the script. About shifting from limiting beliefs to empowering identity. About reclaiming your voice so it serves mission, not fear. About building a self-narrative sturdy enough to withstand pressure without needing armor or theater.

Why the Script Matters

Psychologists call it *self-schema*—the cognitive frameworks we hold about ourselves. Self-schemas guide attention, memory, and decision-making. If your schema is "I'm not a natural leader," your brain unconsciously filters out evidence of influence and overweighs evidence of doubt. If your schema is "My value comes from being perfect," you work twice as hard, but never feel done.

Neuroscience confirms that identity beliefs shape performance. Functional MRI studies show that self-referential processing activates the medial prefrontal cortex (mPFC). When the mPFC engages around negative self-beliefs, the amygdala's threat response intensifies, creating cycles of anxiety and withdrawal. Conversely, affirming empowering identities dampens amygdala activation and engages reward circuits, such as the ventral striatum, which reinforce approach behavior.

Translation: your script isn't just mental—it is neurobiological. A negative identity triggers protective withdrawal; a grounded identity unlocks proactive presence.

The Cost of a Limiting Script

Consider three common limiting scripts leaders carry:

1. **The Proving Script:** *"I'll never be enough unless I keep achieving."*
    - **Outcome:** overwork, burnout, shallow wins

2. **The People-Pleasing Script:** *"My job is to keep everyone happy."*
    - **Outcome:** avoidance of hard feedback, poor boundaries, and team stagnation

3. **The Silence Script:** *"Better to say nothing than risk being wrong."*
    - **Outcome:** missed opportunities, green dashboards hiding red realities

Research supports the cost. A longitudinal study in the *Journal of Applied Psychology* found that leaders with maladaptive self-concepts reported higher stress, lower resilience, and increased turnover intentions. Conversely, leaders who reframed identity around learning and adaptability showed stronger performance and well-being.

Case: In healthcare, junior nurses often default to the silence script—hesitating to question senior physicians. A landmark study in *Critical Care Medicine* found that hierarchical fear was a leading factor in delayed escalation during emergencies. Where leaders normalized humility—"Better to call early and be wrong than late and be right"—response times improved dramatically. Rewriting the script at the individual and system level literally saved lives.

PERSONAL STORY:

The Leader No One Asked For

I still remember sitting in my car after another long day at the pharmaceutical company, staring at the steering wheel with that familiar ache in my chest — the feeling that I was supposed to be leading, yet somehow hadn't been chosen.

It wasn't unfamiliar territory. In the Church of Jesus Christ of Latter-day Saints, leadership is never something you chase. You're called to it. You don't submit an application or raise your hand; someone you trust looks you in the eye and says, "The Lord has called you." When I was asked to serve in a stake presidency, that calling came with both reverence and fear. But it also came with authority — and clarity.

In corporate America, it was different. No one was asking.

I had led hundreds of Marines — young men who would follow me into chaos because they trusted me, or at least they trusted the system. But in the pharmaceutical world, I felt invisible. Promotions came and went. My mind replayed the same silent script:

> "You have to prove you belong. You can't let them see weakness."

So, I pushed harder. Achieved more. Smiled through exhaustion. Each time I hit a milestone, I immediately raised the bar, convinced that real leaders never slowed down, never doubted, never showed cracks.

But the irony was painful: the harder I tried to appear humble, the more hollow it felt.

When you live with imposter syndrome, humility gets twisted. It stops being a strength and becomes submission — something you do to stay small so you won't be "found out." I thought humility meant shrinking. I thought confidence meant pretending.

The cost?

Years of tension between who I was and who I thought I had to be. I worried constantly about how others saw me and what

The Humility Advantage

they thought of me — bosses, peers, even subordinates. I was performing leadership, not living it.

The turning point came slowly — not a single moment of triumph, but a gradual awakening through coaching.

One day, during a client session, I heard myself say words that landed like an echo in my own heart:

> "You can't lead others from a place you haven't learned to lead yourself."

That's when I realized — I'd been waiting for permission that would never come. In the Marines and in the Church, leadership is given. In the corporate world — and in life — true leadership is chosen.

That old script — "You have to be asked to lead" — cracked wide open.

My new script became:

> "I lead by truth-telling, not image management. I don't need a title to lead — I need alignment."

As I rewired my mind through many of the same exercises now in this book — breathwork, mindfulness, Positive Intelligence®, and identity reframing — something shifted.

I stopped hustling for approval. I stopped waiting to be chosen. And for the first time in years, I led with peace instead of pressure.

That rewiring didn't just change how I led — it changed how I lived.

Now, when I coach leaders who struggle with imposter syndrome, I can tell them from experience:

Leadership isn't granted by title or calling. It begins the moment you stop pretending — and decide to lead from within.

Framework: From Limiting Belief to Empowering Identity

Rewriting the script involves four moves:

1. Awareness: Spot the limiting script.

Name the specific belief ("I don't belong in this room").

2. Interruption: Use tools like breathwork or journaling to pause the automatic loop. This is where you're interrupting the nervous system, shifting from the sympathetic nervous system, or fight or flight, to the parasympathetic nervous system, or rest and recover.

3. Replacement: Introduce empowering truths ("I earned this role through experience and skill"). Come up with your own affirmations - see Practice 3 below.

4. Reinforcement: Practice until the new script becomes the default.

This is not motivational fluff; it's behavioral neuroscience. Repetition rewires synaptic pathways through long-term potentiation (LTP)—the biological basis of learning. What you practice, you strengthen.

Practice 1: Journaling as Cognitive Reframing

Writing externalizes thought. It moves limiting beliefs from vague mental fog to visible sentences that can be tested and challenged.

Exercise: The "Two-Column Journal"

- **Column A:** Write the critic's script ("I'm always behind," "I'll fail if I delegate")
- **Column B:** Write the grounded reframe ("I manage priorities; I can delegate without losing control")

This mirrors cognitive-behavioral therapy techniques. A meta-analysis in *Behavior Research and Therapy* shows journaling interventions significantly reduce rumination and increase psychological flexibility.

Leader story: Howard Schultz, former CEO of Starbucks, often wrote in his journals about self doubt after the company's early stumbles. By articulating fear on paper, he created the space to reframe and recommit. His journals became a script-rewriting tool that fueled persistence.

Practice 2: Breathwork for State Reset

Belief work is harder when your body is in threat mode. Breathwork calms the nervous system, lowering cortisol and re-engaging the prefrontal cortex.

Exercise: The Command State Breath

1. Ten rapid belly breaths (inhale and exhale quickly through the nose, focusing on diaphragmatic expansion)

2. End with a double inhale through the nose (short inhale + quick top-off)

3. Hold for two seconds.

4. Exhale slowly through pursed lips—longer than the inhale.

5. Repeat 4–5 times

This sequence activates the parasympathetic nervous system, widening the window of tolerance for stress. Research in *Frontiers in Psychology* confirms that paced breathing increases heart rate variability (HRV), improving emotion regulation and resilience.

Corporate case: At Google, mindfulness and breathwork sessions were integrated into leadership training. Evaluations showed participants reported higher clarity in meetings and reduced reactivity during conflict. Breath wasn't fluff—it was cognitive control in action.

Practice 3: Identity-Based Affirmations

Traditional affirmations sometimes backfire—if the gap between statement and belief is too wide, the brain resists. Identity-based affirmations work differently: they link behaviors to values and growth.

Example:

- **Limiting:** "I'm not confident."
- **Replacement:** "I am a leader who practices calm presence."

Traditional affirmations focus on static traits, while identity-based affirmations focus on ongoing embodiment.

The statement "I'm not confident" is a self-judgment anchored in lack. Its traditional opposite—"I am confident"—often triggers internal resistance because the brain subconsciously scans for evidence and finds contradictions ("No, you weren't confident in that meeting yesterday"). This creates cognitive dissonance and sometimes increases self-doubt.

By contrast, "I am a leader who practices calm presence" is an identity-based affirmation because:

1. It links behavior to identity. You're not claiming a static state ("confident"); you're affirming a way of being ("leader who practices").

2. It invites practice, not perfection. The word "practices" signals growth and self-compassion, aligning with neuroplasticity—the idea that you can change through repetition.

3. It aligns with values. "Calm presence" connects to emotional intelligence and humility, values that the prefrontal cortex easily accepts as aspirational rather than delusional.

4. It lowers resistance. Instead of arguing with your current self-image, your brain recognizes the statement as a plausible identity you're reinforcing through behavior.

Research from the Personality and Social Psychology Bulletin supports this: when affirmations are tied to core values rather than ego ideals, the stress response decreases and problem-solving increases under pressure.

Healthcare example: A study of nursing students showed that identity-based affirmations ("I am someone who learns through challenge") reduced test anxiety and improved performance. The same pattern holds in leadership: reframing identity stabilizes performance under stress.

Practice 4: Focused Visualization

The brain does not perfectly distinguish between vividly imagined scenarios and real ones. Visualization activates many of the same neural circuits as lived experience, including the motor cortex, amygdala, and prefrontal cortex.

We know this because research using functional MRI scans—such as a 2004 study in *Neuropsychologia*—showed that when participants merely imagined performing a physical action, their brains "lit up" in the same motor and sensory regions as when they actually performed the movement.

Exercise: The Leadership Rehearsal

- Close your eyes and visualize the upcoming high-stakes moment

- Imagine yourself entering calm, breathing evenly, naming uncertainty, inviting input
- Repeat daily for one week

Studies in *Neuropsychologia* show that visualization strengthens neural preparedness, while sports psychology research confirms that mental rehearsal improves performance under pressure.

Healthcare example: Surgeons who used visualization before complex procedures reported lower stress and fewer intraoperative errors. If humility is presence, visualization is practice for presence.

Encouragement: Calm Certainty vs. Performative Confidence

Leaders are often told to "fake it till you make it." But performative confidence is brittle. It cracks under scrutiny and alienates teams who sense the act.

Calm certainty is different. It is grounded, not flashy. It comes from rehearsed identity, not borrowed bravado. It says: *"I don't know everything, but I know how to center, listen, and lead."*

Story: Angela Ahrendts, former Apple executive, was often praised for her calm presence. Colleagues noted she never raised her voice or projected bluster. Instead, her steadiness created trust. Her script wasn't "be the loudest," but "be the clearest."

Harvard researcher Amy Cuddy's later work emphasized this point: presence, not performance, is what endures. Teams don't need leaders who act unshakable; they need leaders who are steady enough to admit truth, integrate feedback, and move forward.

Case Studies in Rewriting the Script

Healthcare: A Resident's Shift

A medical resident plagued by impostor thoughts journaled daily for eight weeks, documenting fears before rounds. Over time, she paired each fear with a reframe. Supervisors reported a visible shift: from hesitant silence to steady contributions. Burnout scores dropped, and learning rose.

Aviation: Blameless Postmortems

Airline safety improved not just through checklists but through rewriting the script about error. Instead of "error equals incompetence," the new script became "error equals system signal." That humble reframe turned silence into reporting, saving lives.

Technology: Sundar Pichai at Google

When Sundar Pichai became CEO of Google, he inherited a culture known for brilliant but sometimes ego-driven debate. Pichai's leadership style offered a different script. In interviews and town halls, he's known for phrases like "I could be wrong" and "Help me understand your perspective." He reframed leadership from "having all the answers" to "asking the best questions." This shift toward intellectual humility created space for broader voices and helped Google navigate antitrust scrutiny, AI ethics debates, and organizational restructuring with more internal cohesion than many predicted. The script—from certainty to curiosity—became cultural DNA.

Script Reset in Organizations: From Personal Practice to Cultural Change

An individual leader's script doesn't stay private. Like a tuning fork, it resonates outward, shaping how teams talk, decide, and risk. When leaders reclaim their voice with humility and calm certainty, they give others permission to do the same. Conversely, if leaders cling to limiting scripts, teams adopt them by default.

Case 1: Netflix and the Culture of Candor

Netflix's cultural script shifted from *"keep the boss happy"* to *"say the hard truth fast."* Reed Hastings and Patty McCord modeled vulnerability in executive meetings, admitting blind spots and inviting critique. Over time, candor became institutionalized—embedded in performance reviews, hiring, and strategy.

Case 2: Mayo Clinic's Teaming Norms

In Mayo's surgical units, the old script was *"surgeon knows all."* Leaders rewrote it: *"The patient's life is safest when everyone speaks."* Pre-surgery check-ins, where each team member introduced themselves by name and role, reinforced the new collective identity. Complication rates fell measurably.

Case 3: Ford's Turnaround

When Alan Mulally became CEO in 2006, Ford's executive script was *"Never admit bad news."* Mulally rewrote it immediately, praising rather than punishing the first VP who reported a failure. That single act reshaped the script: *"Telling the truth is how we win."* The company's turnaround followed.

Practical Moves for Script Reset in Organizations

1. Language Audit: Replace fear phrases ("Don't rock the boat") with curiosity-driven alternatives ("What blind spot are we missing?").

2. Symbolic Acts: Micro-behaviors—leaders admitting ignorance, crediting dissent—signal new scripts faster than slogans.

3. Shared Rituals: Blameless postmortems, junior-first speaking orders, or checklists that democratize voice encode the new script through repetition.

4. Storytelling: Retell moments when humility or candor saved the mission. Stories anchor new scripts in memory more than policies ever will.

Leader's Playbook: Rewriting the Script

1. Script Audit (Weekly): Write down one recurring self-limiting phrase. Test it with evidence. Replace with a grounded truth.

Self-limiting phrase: "I'm not technical enough to lead this engineering team."

Evidence test: I've successfully guided three product launches. The team regularly asks for my strategic input. Two engineers told me my questions helped them think differently.

Grounded truth: "I lead through clarity of vision and asking the questions that matter."

2. Breath-Anchor Ritual: Before key meetings, practice three cycles of double inhale/long exhale. Let breath be the bridge to presence.

Before entering the board meeting, you pause outside the door. Inhale through the nose twice (short-short). Exhale slowly through the mouth for eight counts. Repeat three times. The racing thoughts are quiet. You walk in centered, not scrambling.

3. Identity Affirmation Card: Write one identity-based statement aligned with values ("I am a leader who grows by listening"). Keep it visible.

Index card on your desk reads: "I am a leader who creates safety for hard truths." You glance at it before one-on-ones, letting it anchor who you're becoming, not who you fear you are.

4. Visualization Rehearsal: Spend five minutes daily picturing yourself leading from humility and presence.

Each morning with your morning beverage of choice, you close your eyes for five minutes. You see yourself in tomorrow's difficult conversation—listening fully before responding, asking "What am I missing?" without defensiveness, with your shoulders relaxed and your presence steady.

5. Voice Calibration: In one meeting per week, speak early—not to dominate, but to break the silence script.

In the Monday strategy meeting, you typically wait to speak last. This week, after the opening question, you pause three seconds and say: "Here's what I'm thinking…" Not to have the final word—to break your pattern of silence as safety.

6. Celebration Journal: End each day by writing one example of when you showed calm certainty. Repetition encodes identity.

Today's entry: "When Sarah's proposal was criticized, I didn't jump to fix it. I asked three clarifying questions, stayed curious, and let the team work toward the answer. My calm made space for their thinking."

7. Peer Challenge Partner: Share one limiting script with a trusted colleague. Ask them to reflect on the evidence you're overlooking.

You tell your colleague Marcus, "I keep saying 'I'm not creative enough for this role.' Can you point out times when you've seen me solve problems in unexpected ways?" He reminds you of four instances you'd completely dismissed.

8. Team Script Check: In your next staff meeting, ask: "What's one phrase or belief that holds this team back?" Use the moment to begin a collective rewrite.

Mid-meeting, you pause the agenda: "I want to try something. What's one phrase or belief we keep repeating that might be limiting us?" After the silence, someone says, "We always say we're too small to compete." The room shifts. You write it on the whiteboard and ask, "What if that's not actually true?"

Reflection Prompt #6

Write the current script that holds you back. Be brutally honest: what words echo before you speak, decide, or lead?

Now rewrite it. Draft the script you want to carry—one rooted in calm certainty and grounded worth. Say it aloud once a day this week. Notice how the room feels when you lead from the new script.

Chapter Takeaway

Rewriting the script is not a one-time exercise. It is daily authorship. Each breath, each journal line, each affirmation is a sentence in the new story you're telling about who you are as a leader.

The old script says: *Stay quiet. Play small. Protect yourself.*

The new script says: *Stand steady. Speak truth. Serve the mission.*

Humility doesn't erase your voice; it reclaims it. Calm certainty isn't louder—it's clearer.

Bridge to Chapter 7

If Chapter 6 was about rewriting your inner script, Chapter 7 is about embodying it in every interaction. Once you reclaim your voice, the next step is to show up with it consistently—leading from your center rather than your wounds.

Chapter 7: Centered Leadership—Wisdom Over Wounds will explore how humble leaders cultivate clarity, courage, and consistency. How they move from reactive leadership (ego-driven, wound-triggered) to centered leadership (values-driven, grounded in truth). This is where the inner transformation becomes outer presence.

The gold is emerging. Let's keep chipping away.

Join our community

Chapter 7
Centered Leadership— Wisdom Over Wounds

When leaders are praised for being "centered," what people are really noticing is stability under pressure.

They see clarity where others panic, courage where others retreat, and consistency where others swing between extremes. But here's what most leadership development misses: you can't teach centeredness through techniques alone. Centered leaders don't deny difficulty—they meet it from a deeper foundation, one that can only be accessed by removing the clay layers that keep them reactive, defensive, and wound-driven.

This chapter is about leading from the center. It is about cultivating clarity, courage, and consistency, not by erasing fear but by anchoring identity beyond it. It is about shifting from wounded reactions—ego, defensiveness, over-control— to wisdom-driven responses—listening, discernment, calm strength. And it is about how humility unlocks the very capacity to lead with confident presence.

Leading from the Center: Three Anchors

Centered leadership is not a personality trait; it is a cultivated posture. Three anchors define it:

1. **Clarity** — the ability to see what matters without distortion
2. **Courage** — the willingness to act in alignment with values even when uncertain
3. **Consistency** — the discipline of showing up the same way across contexts, so others can trust your presence as much as your words

These anchors don't emerge automatically. They require humility because clarity demands admitting bias, courage demands openness to risk, and consistency demands discipline over ego.

Clarity: Seeing Through the Noise

Clarity is more than information; it is perception free from the ego's fog. Neuroscience sheds light here.

- **Cognitive Load:** Under stress, working memory shrinks. Leaders over-focused on image, spending bandwidth protecting ego instead of analyzing data.
- **Bias Interruption:** Humility supports metacognition —the ability to notice one's own thinking. Research in *Organizational Behavior and Human Decision Processes* shows leaders who acknowledge limits are better at integrating diverse perspectives and reducing bias.
- **Emotional Clarity:** Leaders high in emotional intelligence, particularly self-awareness, demonstrate greater accuracy in reading both their own emotions and others'. This allows them to separate fact from fear.

Case example: Healthcare. During the SARS outbreak in Toronto, one hospital leader was described by colleagues as "a calm lens in the chaos." While others rushed to assign blame or overpromise safety, she centered the team by naming what was known, what was uncertain, and what would be reviewed daily. That clarity—humble enough to admit limits—reduced panic and improved compliance with evolving protocols.

Clarity flows not from pretending to know, but from admitting what you don't and focusing on what matters most.

Courage: Acting Without Certainty

Courage in leadership isn't reckless bravado. It is the willingness to act when outcomes aren't guaranteed. And humility strengthens courage by freeing leaders from the need to protect their ego.

- **Moral Courage:** A 2021 study in the *Journal of Business Ethics* found leaders with higher humility scores were more likely to engage in ethical voice—speaking up against misconduct even at personal cost.
- **Risk-Taking Courage:** Research in the *Academy of Management Journal* shows that teams led by humble leaders are more innovative, because psychological safety emboldens risk-taking.
- **Interpersonal Courage:** Courage often means entering tough conversations—giving feedback, naming conflict, or admitting error. Humility lowers the perceived threat of these acts, reframing them as service to mission, not self-exposure.

Aviation example. In 2009, Captain Chesley "Sully" Sullenberger embodied courageous humility. When both engines failed over New York, he didn't react with ego or denial. He calmly told air traffic control: *"We're going to be in the Hudson."* That decision—neither arrogant fantasy nor fearful freeze—saved 155 lives. His courage was anchored in presence, not panic.

Courage from the center is not loud. It is steady.

Consistency: Stability Others Can Trust

Consistency is the gift leaders give their teams when they stop being ruled by moods or wounds. It is the lived pattern of predictable values under unpredictable conditions.

- **Trust Research:** A study in *Leadership Quarterly* found that consistency of leader behavior predicted trust more strongly than charisma or intelligence. Employees described inconsistent leaders as "dangerous," because unpredictability heightened stress.
- **Neurobiology:** Consistency regulates team stress. When leaders remain steady, subordinates' cortisol levels drop, enabling better performance under strain.
- **Authenticity:** Consistency flows from aligning inner identity with outward behavior. Leaders who perform one script in public and another in private exhaust themselves and confuse others.

Corporate case: Sundar Pichai's leadership at Google is repeatedly described as consistent. He listens the same way in a town hall as in the boardroom. He acknowledges mistakes in public as readily as in private. This steadiness contrasts sharply with cultures where teams waste energy predicting which version of the boss will walk in.

Consistency is not monotone; it is trustworthiness.

Humility: The Gateway to Center

Clarity, courage, and consistency all rest on humility. Without humility, clarity turns into stubbornness, courage turns into recklessness, and consistency turns into rigidity.

Humility allows leaders to:

- Listen without defensiveness
- Admit uncertainty without collapse
- Hold presence without over-identifying with status

It is humility that makes centered leadership possible, because only a humble leader can step out of ego's noise long enough to hear wisdom.

Wisdom Over Wounds

Every leader carries wounds—moments of rejection, humiliation, or failure that left an imprint. Unexamined, those wounds dictate scripts: *prove yourself, hide mistakes, control everything.*

Centered leadership doesn't mean erasing wounds. It means learning from them without letting them drive.

- **Post-Traumatic Growth Research:** A meta-analysis in *Psychological Bulletin* shows that individuals who process past adversity with openness often develop greater wisdom, empathy, and resilience. The wound becomes compost for wisdom.
- **Narrative Reframing:** Leaders who reframe failures as sources of learning exhibit higher resilience and lower burnout (*Journal of Occupational Health Psychology*, 2019).

Military example: General James Mattis often spoke about "learning to carry scars with discipline." Instead of letting combat wounds (literal and psychological) dictate reactivity, he cultivated a reputation for calm, bookish reflection—his "library card" was as important as his rifle. His wisdom emerged not by denying wounds but by integrating them.

Wisdom over wounds is the essence of centered leadership.

Detachment from Ego: Eastern Insights

The Dhammapada, an ancient Buddhist text, teaches: "As a solid rock is not shaken by the wind, the wise are not moved by praise or blame."

This is centered leadership described centuries before neuroscience: detachment from ego. Not indifference, but freedom. When a leader's identity is not tied to praise or blame, they can focus on the mission rather than self-protection.

How does a leader practice detachment? By noticing the moment the ego gets hooked—the flash of defensiveness when challenged, the hunger for credit after a win, the contraction when someone else shines. The practice is not to eliminate these reactions but to observe them without feeding them. Name the feeling: "There's my ego wanting protection." Then return to the question that matters: "What does this moment require of me?" *Detachment is built through repetition—catching the ego's pull, loosening its grip, and redirecting attention back to purpose.*

Eastern traditions consistently link humility with clarity:

- Non-Attachment (Buddhism): Leaders detach from ego-driven craving for validation
- Wu Wei (Taoism): Leading without force, allowing flow instead of over-control
- Zen Practice: Returning again and again to the present moment, where reactivity cannot dominate

Modern research echoes this. A study in the *Mindfulness* journal (2016) found that leaders who practiced non-attachment reported higher well-being, lower burnout, and stronger follower ratings of authenticity. Detachment is not withdrawal—it is liberation from the ego's grip.

Practices for Centered Leadership

1. The Centering Breath

Adapted from mindfulness traditions and Navy SEAL training:

- Inhale for four counts
- Hold for four counts

- Exhale for six counts
- Hold for two counts

Repeat three times before a high-stakes interaction. This balances the nervous system and primes presence.

2. The "Wisdom Over Wounds" Journal

Write one wound-driven script that echoes in your leadership (e.g., "Don't let anyone see weakness"). Then rewrite it as wisdom: "Strength is making space for others' voices." Repeat weekly.

3. The Non-Reactivity Cue

Pick a small anchor (touching your pen, taking a sip of water). Each time you feel triggered, use the cue to pause before responding. Over time, the pause becomes a habit.

4. Detachment Practice

At the end of the day, ask: *"Where did I react to praise or blame today?"* Note it without judgment. With repetition, your identity shifts from performance to presence.

Case Studies: Centered Leadership in Action

Healthcare: The COVID-19 ICUs

During the height of the pandemic, ICUs faced unprecedented strain. Leaders who stayed centered—naming fear, grounding decisions in values, and keeping routines consistent—were rated by staff as more trustworthy. A *BMJ Open* study confirmed that a leader's calmness was strongly correlated with lower staff burnout scores.

Aviation: Crew Resource Management

CRM rewrote aviation's cultural script from hierarchy to centered communication. Captains were retrained to listen without ego, creating space for co-pilots' voices. Accident rates dropped dramatically.

Corporate: Indra Nooyi at PepsiCo

Nooyi combined humility with centered clarity. She famously wrote personal letters to the parents of her executives, acknowledging the families behind the leaders. This act was both humble and consistent with her centered belief: business is built on people, not just profit. Under her tenure, PepsiCo's revenues doubled.

Nonprofit: The Dalai Lama

Asked how he maintains joy despite exile, he said: *"I practice accepting reality as it is, not as I wish it to be."* His leadership, grounded in detachment from ego, continues to mobilize millions without reactivity.

The Centered Leader's Playbook

1. Daily Centering: Begin the day with a breath or meditation practice to anchor before emails and meetings.

Example: Maria, a department head, wakes at 6:30 AM and sits in her home office for 10 minutes before touching her phone. She does box breathing (4 counts in, 4 hold, 4 out, 4 hold) while repeating a grounding phrase: "I lead from calm, not chaos." Only after this does she open her laptop. On days she skips this, she notices she reacts to the first urgent email with tension that colors her entire morning.

2. Wisdom Journaling: Reframe one wound-driven script weekly into a wisdom statement.

Example: James notices he often interrupts colleagues in meetings, a pattern rooted in childhood, where he had to fight for attention among four siblings. His wound-driven script: "If I don't speak loudly and quickly, I won't be heard." He reframes this into wisdom: "My voice has weight because I listen deeply first. I create space for others, which makes my contributions land with more impact." He writes this in his journal and reviews it before Monday's leadership meetings.

3. Feedback Ritual: In tense conversations, begin with: "Here's what I may not see." This disarms the ego and signals humility.

Example: During a budget dispute with her CFO, Sarah feels her jaw tighten and defensiveness rising. Instead of justifying her department's request, she pauses and says: "Here's what I may not see—I might be so focused on my team's needs that I'm missing the broader financial constraints you're navigating. Help me understand your perspective." The CFO's shoulders drop, and the conversation shifts from a positional to a collaborative approach.

4. Consistency Audit: Ask colleagues privately: "Do I show up the same in pressure as in calm?" Track patterns.

Example: David asks three trusted colleagues separately: "I want to grow as a leader. Do I show up the same way when we're hitting our targets as when we're behind? Be honest." Two mentions, he becomes curt and stops making eye contact during stressful quarters. He tracks this for a month, noting when pressure makes him withdraw. He commits to one extra check-in per week during high-stress periods to counteract the pattern.

5. Non-Attachment Check: Notice when praise inflates you, or criticism crushes you. Name it. Re-anchor in values.

Example: After presenting to the executive team, Keisha receives praise from the CEO: "Brilliant work." She notices her chest swelling, her inner voice saying, "I'm finally legitimate." Two hours later, she catches herself: "I'm attaching my worth to his approval." She writes in her notes: "My value isn't created by praise or destroyed by criticism. I'm anchored in my commitment to clear thinking and ethical service." The inflation deflates; she returns to baseline.

6. Team Reflection: End meetings with a centering question: "What truth emerged today that we need to carry forward?"

Example: At the end of a tense strategy meeting where the team debated killing an underperforming product line, the leader doesn't immediately adjourn. Instead, she asks: "What truth emerged today that we need to carry forward?" After silence, someone says, "That we've been avoiding this decision for six months because we're attached to the founder's vision, not because the data supports it." Another adds: "That killing something can be an act of integrity, not failure." The leader writes both on the whiteboard: "These are our guideposts now."

Reflection Prompt #7

Think of a recent moment when you were triggered by either praise or blame. Write the script you wanted to run. Then write the wiser script you wish to embody. Commit to practicing that script in your next leadership moment.

Chapter Takeaway

Centered leadership is not the absence of fear or flaw. It is the discipline of standing steady in the middle of both. It is clarity in uncertainty, courage in ambiguity, and consistency in turbulence. It is humility's gift: the freedom to listen without defensiveness, to act without arrogance, to lead without over-identifying with ego.

The wounds will always whisper. But wisdom speaks louder when humility anchors the center.

Bridge to Chapter 8

If Chapter 7 described the posture of centered leadership, Chapter 8 will explore its most visible expression: **Quiet Confidence—How to Speak Up Without Arrogance or Shrinking**. Because once you're centered, the question becomes: how do you speak from that place? How do you develop a voice that commands attention not by demanding it, but by radiating steadiness?

The inner work continues to become an outer presence.

Chapter 8
Quiet Confidence—How to Speak Up Without Arrogance or Shrinking

Most leaders swing between two extremes: shrinking when uncertain, posturing when pressured. But the highest-performing leaders live in a different zone altogether.

Confidence in leadership is a paradox. Too little, and you fade into the background. Too much, and you overpower the room. Most leaders swing between the two: shrinking when uncertain, posturing when pressured. But the highest-performing leaders live in a different zone altogether. They embody quiet confidence—a presence that communicates authority without arrogance and openness without self-erasure.

Quiet confidence is not volume, charisma, or dominance. It is a posture. It is the balance of conviction and humility, clarity and curiosity. It is the ability to speak up in a way that commands attention, not because it demands it, but because it radiates steadiness.

This chapter explores the anatomy of quiet confidence: how leaders develop presence without pretense, how they use language and posture to signal authority and openness, and how they receive feedback with curiosity instead of defensiveness.

Leadership Presence Without Pretense

Leadership presence has been studied across domains—from corporate boardrooms to operating rooms. The data show that presence matters as much as content.

- **Voice of Calm:** Research in the *Journal of Applied Psychology* shows that leaders who speak at a measured pace and with a lower vocal pitch are rated as more competent and trustworthy, regardless of the content. Quiet confidence often communicates more than loud certainty.
- **Body Signals:** Newer studies confirm that posture communicates. A 2019 study in *Leadership Quarterly* found that expansive but relaxed body language increased perceptions of warmth and competence more than aggressive expansiveness.
- **Non-Defensive Presence:** Presence is not just projection—it is reception. A 2020 *Harvard Business Review* survey found that employees rated leaders as most present when they listened without interrupting and made eye contact, not when they filled airtime.

Personal story: I was a young captain serving as the commanding officer of a company of Marines. This was an unusual company because it was a training company. Marines came to me from basic training and received their military occupational specialty (MOS). Another unique characteristic of this company was that the leader of one of the schools, which had four schools, was a Master Gunnery Sergeant, E-9. I heard him watch a Marine walk across a large open non-combat field and say, "You can tell just by the way that

Marine walks that people won't want to follow him." That's presence displayed in the Marine's posture as he walked.

Healthcare case: During a code-blue emergency, teams look to the physician in charge. Research in *Critical Care Medicine* shows that physicians rated as calm and directive—clear commands, measured tone—had higher survival rates in resuscitation scenarios. Quiet confidence literally saves lives.

Corporate story: When Warren Buffett addresses shareholders, his calm tone and simple language convey authority without theatrics. He doesn't posture; he steadies. His presence demonstrates that confidence isn't noise—it's clarity plus credibility.

Language and Posture that Communicate Both Authority and Openness

Words matter. So does how you deliver them. Quietly confident leaders combine clear authority with genuine openness.

Authority Through Clarity

Authority doesn't require force. It requires clarity.

- **Direct Statements:** "Here is what we know. Here is what we don't. Here is what I recommend. What am I missing?"
- **Short Sentences:** Long, hedging explanations dilute authority.
- **Values Anchoring:** Framing decisions through values communicates principled confidence: "We'll prioritize patient safety above speed."

Openness Through Curiosity

Openness is conveyed not by disclaimers but by curiosity.

- **Inviting Input:** "What perspective am I missing?"
- **Acknowledging Risk:** "Here are the uncertainties. How do you see them?"
- **Crediting Others:** Publicly recognizing contributions signals both humility and strength.

Tech case: When Jensen Huang leads Nvidia executive meetings, he's known for the phrase "I don't know" followed by "Help me understand." This linguistic pattern reframes authority as collaborative rather than dictatorial. That shift toward intellectual humility has helped Nvidia dominate the AI chip market by creating a culture where truth-telling and rapid iteration became competitive advantages.

Posture Matters

Physiological research shows that open posture—shoulders relaxed, hands visible, head upright—activates mirror neurons in others that prime trust. In contrast, defensive posture (crossed arms, tense jaw) triggers suspicion. Leaders' bodies speak even when their mouths are silent.

The Neuroscience of Postural Signaling

Mirror neurons, discovered in the 1990s, fire both when we perform an action and when we observe someone else performing it. This neural mechanism creates a form of embodied empathy—when you see someone's shoulders drop in relaxation, your own nervous system begins to mirror that state. Research in *Social Cognitive and Affective*

Neuroscience (2010) demonstrated that observing open, relaxed postures activates the ventromedial prefrontal cortex, a brain region associated with safety and social reward. Conversely, observing closed or tense postures activates the amygdala, the brain's threat-detection system.

What Open Posture Communicates

Trust signals: Visible hands (palms occasionally open, not hidden in pockets or clenched) have evolutionary roots—they signal "I'm not concealing a weapon." In modern contexts, this translates to psychological safety: "I have nothing to hide."

Cognitive accessibility: An upright but relaxed head position suggests alertness without hypervigilance. It signals "I'm here, present, and available" rather than "I'm scanning for threats" (head darting) or "I'm checked out" (head down, slumped).

Emotional regulation: Relaxed shoulders communicate that the leader is not bracing for an attack. A 2018 study in *Emotion* found that participants who observed leaders with chronically raised shoulders (a freeze response) rated them as less competent and more anxious, even when facial expressions were neutral.

What Defensive Posture Reveals

Crossed arms: While often habitual or comfortable, crossed arms are universally interpreted as a barrier. Research from the *International Journal of Research in Marketing* (2013) showed that negotiators with crossed arms were 30% less likely to reach an agreement, even when their verbal proposals were identical to those with open arms.

Tense jaw/clenched teeth: Microexpressions of jaw tension signal suppressed anger or fear. Team members unconsciously pick up on this and become guarded. A study in *The Leadership Quarterly* (2017) found that leaders with visible jaw tension during feedback sessions received less honest input from direct reports.

Collapsed or hunched posture: Shoulders rolled forward, and chest collapsed signal defeat or shame. This posture reduces lung capacity and oxygen flow, creating a feedback loop—the leader feels less energized, which reinforces the defeated posture. Team members mirror this, and collective energy drops.

The Feedback Loop: Your Posture Changes Your State

Amy Cuddy's research on "power posing" has been debated, but the core finding remains robust: posture affects hormones and self-perception. A 2017 meta-analysis in *Psychological Bulletin* confirmed that adopting expansive postures for even two minutes increases feelings of power and reduces cortisol. Leaders who intentionally adjust their posture before high-stakes moments—standing tall, opening the chest, releasing the shoulders—report feeling more grounded and thinking more clearly.

Practical Application

Pre-meeting centering: Before entering a room, take three deep breaths. On the exhale, consciously drop your shoulders away from your ears. Roll your head gently. Let your jaw soften. This 30-second practice signals to your nervous system (and everyone watching) that you're entering from a place of calm authority, not survival mode.

The Humility Advantage

The "caught posture" check: Throughout the day, pause and notice: How am I holding myself right now? Is my jaw tight? Are my shoulders by my ears? Am I crossing my arms? Simply noticing breaks the automatic pattern. Reset to open, grounded posture.

Model what you want to see: If you want your team to be open and collaborative, your body must model it first. Sit back rather than leaning aggressively forward. Keep arms uncrossed during conflict. Maintain a relaxed, upright spine. Teams will unconsciously match your postural tone.

The Silent Authority of the Body

In high-stakes environments—trauma bays, boardrooms, cockpits—the leader's posture often matters more than their words. A surgeon who enters an operating room with hurried, tense movements spreads anxiety through the surgical team. A CEO who sits through an earnings call with crossed arms and a rigid spine signals defensiveness, even if their verbal message is optimistic. The body cannot lie for long. Leaders who cultivate postural awareness create a somatic foundation for trust that words alone can never build.

Bottom line: Your posture is your team's thermostat. You set the nervous system temperature of the room before you say a single word.

Aviation example: In post-flight crew evaluations, captains who leaned forward, made eye contact, and acknowledged co-pilots' input were rated significantly higher on leadership effectiveness. Their words mattered less than their posture of openness.

Political example: Margaret Thatcher's communication style was notably direct and unyielding. Her clipped delivery, firm hand gestures, and unwavering eye contact projected absolute conviction. She seldom hedged her statements with qualifiers; her certainty was the message itself, whether addressing Parliament or facing down critics.

Receiving Feedback with Curiosity, Not Defensiveness

Feedback is the crucible of quiet confidence. Leaders who react with defensiveness communicate fragility, not strength. Leaders who receive feedback with curiosity communicate confidence, secure enough to grow.

- **Neuroscience:** fMRI studies show that criticism activates the anterior cingulate cortex (ACC)—the brain's error-detection system. For defensive leaders, this triggers amygdala reactivity, leading to fight-or-flight. Humble leaders engage the prefrontal cortex to reframe feedback as data rather than threat.
- **Organizational Impact:** A 2019 *MIT Sloan Management Review* article found that teams with leaders who responded openly to feedback had 31% higher engagement scores. Teams mirrored the leader's openness.
- **Personal Growth:** Research in the *Journal of Organizational Behavior* shows that feedback-seeking behavior correlates with higher leadership effectiveness, but only when coupled with humility. Without humility, feedback-seeking can feel manipulative.

Military case: In the U.S. Marine Corps, after-action reviews institutionalize a culture of reflection and learning. These structured discussions help Marines identify what went right, what went wrong, and how to improve future performance. Leaders facilitate open, blame-free dialogue to promote collective insight and continuous improvement. Units that conduct thorough, honest AARs consistently adapt faster and strengthen trust within their teams.

Corporate example: Indra Nooyi, former CEO of PepsiCo, was known for asking, "What am I missing?" in strategy sessions. Her openness didn't undercut authority—it deepened it. Employees reported greater loyalty because they felt their voice mattered.

Why Arrogance and Shrinking Are Two Sides of the Same Coin

Arrogance and shrinking seem opposite, but both are ego-driven.

- **Arrogance:** Inflated self-presentation to cover insecurity
- **Shrinking:** Withdrawing voice to avoid exposure

In both cases, the script is a form of self-protection. Quiet confidence transcends ego's noise. It's not about *you*—it's about the mission and the people you serve.

Healthcare illustration: A 2022 study in *BMJ Leader* found that physicians who displayed arrogance silenced junior staff, while those who shrank into passivity left decisions unclear. Both patterns harmed outcomes. Teams rated leaders with balanced humility and confidence as most effective.

Philosophical anchor: The *Dhammapada* reminds us: *"Do not be concerned with who praises or blames you. Walk the path with balance."* Eastern wisdom here aligns with modern leadership science: detachment from ego liberates leaders to speak from clarity rather than fear or vanity.

The Science of Quiet Confidence

What makes quiet confidence so compelling isn't just a matter of perception or social convention—it's rooted in our biology. When someone communicates with calm authority, they're triggering specific neurochemical responses in those around them. Understanding these mechanisms reveals why certain communication patterns consistently outperform others, regardless of cultural context.

Hormonal Signaling

- **Oxytocin:** Humble listening elevates oxytocin in others, reinforcing trust
- **Cortisol:** Defensive reactivity spikes cortisol; quiet confidence lowers it through calm presence
- **Testosterone Balance:** Research in Proceedings of the National Academy of Sciences suggests leaders with balanced testosterone and cortisol profiles—assertive but not stressed—are most effective. Quiet confidence reflects this balance: firm but calm.

Emotional Intelligence

A meta-analysis in the *Journal of Vocational Behavior* found emotional intelligence predicted leadership effectiveness across sectors, especially when combined with humility. Leaders who could regulate ego-driven defensiveness showed greater influence and stronger team climates.

Historical Anchors of Quiet Confidence

History offers examples of leaders whose quiet confidence shaped nations and movements.

- **Abraham Lincoln:** Known for calm deliberation and a steady tone, even in a national crisis. His ability to speak plainly yet firmly won both respect and trust.

- **Eleanor Roosevelt:** Initially shy, she developed a steady, confident public presence. Her calm voice during World War II broadcasts reassured millions.

- **Nelson Mandela:** After 27 years in prison, Mandela emerged not with loud rage but with steady calm. His quiet confidence enabled reconciliation instead of revenge.

In each case, the strength wasn't in dominating volume, but in radiating steadiness rooted in humility and conviction.

Practices for Cultivating Quiet Confidence

1. The Clarity Script

Before a meeting, write three short sentences:

- What I know
- What I don't know
- What I recommend

Deliver these first. It centers authority without arrogance.

2. The Curiosity Cue

End each statement with one open-ended question. Example: "Here's my view. What am I missing?" This signals openness without surrendering authority.

3. Feedback Reframe

When criticized, mentally replace "attack" with "data." Ask: "What signal can I use from this?" Over time, this rewires the ACC-amygdala loop toward curiosity.

4. Body Scan Reset

Before entering a room, pause. Drop shoulders, unclench jaw, breathe evenly. This signals steadiness.

5. Micro-Gratitude Practice

When someone challenges you, thank them aloud. "That's helpful—thank you." Gratitude disarms defensiveness and models strength.

6. Assertive but Humble Scripts

Borrowed from aviation and healthcare:

- "I may be wrong, but I'm concerned about..."
- "Can we double-check this step?"
- "Would you mind reviewing my work on this? I want a second set of eyes."

These scripts communicate both confidence and openness.

7. Posture Check-In

Ask a trusted colleague: "Do I look defensive when challenged?" Awareness precedes change.

Case Studies in Quiet Confidence

Healthcare: The Resident Who Spoke Up

In one ICU, a resident noticed a dosage error but hesitated to speak, fearing rebuke. After training in "assertive but respectful" scripts, she quietly said, "Doctor, may I clarify the dosage?" The correction saved the patient. The attending later praised her calm confidence. Research shows structured communication protocols like **SBAR (Situation-Background-Assessment-Recommendation)** empower a quiet but effective voice.

Aviation: First Officers' Voice

Historically, co-pilots were silent in the face of captain error, leading to disasters like Tenerife (1977). Crew Resource Management rewrote the script. First officers were trained to voice concerns firmly but respectfully. Accident rates plummeted. Quiet confidence—clear voice without arrogance—became industry standard.

Corporate: Mary Barra at GM

When Mary Barra became CEO, she faced the ignition switch crisis. Instead of deflecting or blustering, she spoke with steady clarity: "We failed to do our job. We will take responsibility." Her tone was calm, not defensive. This quiet confidence steadied GM during its most precarious moment.

Nonprofit: Malala Yousafzai

Malala Yousafzai, the youngest Nobel Prize laureate and Pakistani advocate for girls, speaks with quiet confidence. She does not shout; she speaks steadily. Her authority flows from conviction and humility. Neuroscience would say her calm presence regulates listeners' nervous systems, creating trust.

Political: Jacinda Ardern

As New Zealand's prime minister during the Christchurch shooting, Ardern's quiet confidence was evident. She didn't shout or posture. She spoke clearly, embraced grieving families, and modeled openness. Global observers praised her calm conviction as a model for crisis leadership.

Leader's Playbook: Quiet Confidence

1. Presence Audit: Ask a trusted peer: Do I shrink in silence or posture with arrogance? Where do you see it?

2. Voice Calibration: In your next meeting, aim for measured tone, short sentences, and one open invitation for feedback.

3. Feedback Ritual: When criticized, write down three possible truths in the comment before reacting. Shirzad Chamine, author of *Positive Intelligence*, suggests that anything, no matter how outrageous, can be 10 percent useful.

4. Posture Practice: Video yourself in a meeting. Review for signals of defensiveness (crossed arms, clenched jaw) vs. openness (eye contact, relaxed shoulders).

5. Daily Detachment: At day's end, ask: "Did I act from ego today or from mission?" Re-anchor tomorrow.

6. The SBAR Rehearsal: Use structured scripts for high-stakes voice. Practice them until they become natural.

7. Confidence Journal: Each night, write one moment when you spoke with clarity and one when you stayed silent. Track patterns.

Reflection Prompt #8

Think of a time you stayed silent when you had something valuable to add. What script held you back? Now imagine yourself speaking with quiet confidence—what would you have said, and how would you have delivered it? Write it down. Practice saying it aloud.

Chapter Takeaway

Quiet confidence is not about being loud or invisible. It is about being present enough to speak with clarity, humble enough to invite input, and steady enough to receive feedback without flinching.

Arrogance is brittle. Shrinking is costly. Quiet confidence is durable. It steadies rooms, clarifies missions, and multiplies trust.

Bridge to Chapter 9

If Chapter 8 explored the individual art of quiet confidence, Chapter 9 will explore the collective impact of centered, humble leadership on organizational resilience. Because confidence that is quiet but steady doesn't just change how you speak—it reshapes how teams listen, risk, and thrive.

Part III: Leadership from the Center

Chapter 9
Building Resilient Teams with Emotional Clarity
Resilience is no longer a "nice-to-have" in leadership—it's the price of survival.

Organizations today face relentless disruption: pandemics, technological upheavals, staffing crises, and economic swings that would have been unthinkable a decade ago. What distinguishes teams that endure from those that collapse under this pressure? Not raw intelligence or elegant strategy. It's collective resilience—the capacity to adapt, recover, and grow stronger under stress. And that resilience begins with a leader's emotional clarity.

And resilience does not emerge by accident. It is cultivated, moment by moment, through leadership that builds trust, emotional clarity, and shared ownership. At the center of this capacity is humility. Leaders who admit limits, invite voice, and regulate their own emotions signal safety. That safety becomes the soil where teams speak up, innovate, and remain loyal when conditions get tough.

Humble Leadership as the Foundation

A landmark study by Owens & Hekman (2012) found that humble leaders foster greater engagement, stronger collaboration, and higher job satisfaction. Their data showed that humility predicted trust and innovation across industries.

Why? Because humility signals: *"This is not about me. It's about us."*

- **Trust:** Teams trust leaders who acknowledge mistakes and credit others. Trust lowers defensive energy and frees bandwidth for problem-solving.
- **Innovation:** When leaders admit uncertainty, they normalize experimentation. Teams are more willing to propose ideas when failure isn't punished.
- **Retention:** A 2021 study in the *Journal of Nursing Management* found that humble leadership predicted lower turnover among nurses. Leaders who made space for others' voices reduced burnout and strengthened a sense of belonging.

Case example: Mayo Clinic. Senior physicians who modeled humility—thanking nurses for corrections, inviting questions—were rated as more effective. Their teams reported higher safety culture scores and lower turnover intentions.

Humble leadership is disciplined strength—leading with confidence anchored in service, not ego.

Emotional Clarity: The Multiplier

Resilience depends not just on humility but on emotional clarity—the ability to name and regulate emotions in ways that stabilize others. Emotional clarity has three components:

1. **Self-Awareness:** Recognizing your own emotional state before it leaks onto the team

2. **Self-Regulation:** Managing stress and reactivity so others don't have to manage you
3. **Empathic Transparency:** Naming team emotions aloud ("I sense fatigue," "We're frustrated") in ways that normalize and validate

Research in the *Journal of Organizational Behavior* (Miao et al., 2018) shows that emotionally intelligent leaders increase team performance by fostering psychological safety and reducing destructive conflict. Emotional clarity amplifies humble leadership by making space for contribution without fear.

Healthcare story: In one ICU, a leader began rounds with a simple check-in: "How is everyone's energy today?" Staff reported that naming emotions made it safe to admit fatigue. Errors declined. Resilience rose.

How Humility Creates Space for Contribution

Humility doesn't just protect egos—it expands the playing field. When leaders model vulnerability, teams feel permission to contribute without needing to be perfect.

The Voice Effect

Amy Edmondson's psychological safety research shows that teams with higher safety are more likely to surface risks, learn faster, and adapt effectively. Humility fuels safety because it tells the truth: *"I don't know everything. I need your input."*

Aviation example: Crew Resource Management (CRM) rewrote cockpit culture. Captains were trained to replace dominance with inclusive authority: "What do you see?" This humility-based posture reduced accidents dramatically.

The Innovation Effect

Google's Project Aristotle found that the #1 predictor of team effectiveness was psychological safety—created not by star performers but by leaders who modeled humility: listening equally, encouraging turn-taking, and rewarding candor. Innovation was a byproduct of humble climates.

The Retention Effect

A 2022 Gallup survey revealed that employees who feel their voice matters are 4.6 times more likely to stay. Humble leadership is the gateway to voice—and therefore to retention.

Team-Building Rituals that Reinforce Resilience

Resilient teams don't just talk about values—they practice them through rituals. Rituals turn humble leadership into collective muscle memory.

1. The Check-In Circle

Begin meetings with a one-word check-in: "What's your state right now?" This simple ritual lowers cortisol, signals care, and normalizes emotion. A *Harvard Business Review* article (2019) noted that check-ins improve group cohesion by up to 25%.

Healthcare example: ICU teams who added daily emotional check-ins reported lower burnout and higher teamwork scores.

2. The Red Team Drill

Borrowed from military strategy, this ritual assigns a subgroup to challenge assumptions. Humble leaders invite critique not as a threat but as a safeguard. This turns dissent into contribution.

Corporate example: At Amazon, "red teams" test proposals for blind spots. Jeff Bezos institutionalized humility by making critique part of the process.

3. Blameless Postmortems

After errors, teams gather to review what happened without finger-pointing. This ritual reframes error as data, not incompetence. Psychological safety skyrockets.

Aviation example: After every flight incident, crews conduct debriefs emphasizing systems, not personal blame. This ritual made aviation one of the safest industries in the world.

4. Gratitude Rounds

At the end of a week, each team member names one contribution from a peer. Gratitude rituals increase oxytocin, build trust, and buffer stress.

Tech example: At Pixar, "notes sessions" combine critique with gratitude, ensuring feedback strengthens rather than weakens bonds.

5. Assumption Logging

Teams keep a running log of key assumptions behind decisions. Reviewing logs prevents overconfidence and normalizes humility: "Here's where we might be wrong."

Military example: U.S. Marine Corps war-gaming includes explicit assumption tracking, reducing surprises in combat.

6. Micro-Recovery Breaks

Research in *Occupational Health Science* shows that micro-breaks (2–5 minutes of stretching, breathing, or walking) reduce fatigue and increase team engagement. Leaders who normalize breaks send a powerful message: resilience requires recovery, not just effort.

Sports analogy: NBA teams that use strategic timeouts to reset emotional energy often outperform statistically stronger teams. The pause restores clarity.

The Neuroscience of Team Resilience

Resilient teams regulate not just tasks but nervous systems.

- **Cortisol Contagion:** Stress spreads through mirror neurons. A defensive leader spikes team cortisol; a centered leader lowers it.
- **Oxytocin Release:** Trust-building rituals (gratitude, voice, vulnerability) increase oxytocin, which strengthens collaboration.
- **Prefrontal Synchrony:** Teams in flow exhibit synchronized brainwave patterns in the prefrontal cortex, enabling coordinated action. Humble leadership catalyzes this synchrony by reducing ego noise.

Neuroleadership study: Rock & Ringleb (2020) found that leaders who practiced mindfulness and humility produced measurable drops in team stress biomarkers. Emotional clarity is contagious.

Additional Case Studies in Resilient Teams

Healthcare: The Keystone ICU Project

By empowering nurses to stop procedures if protocols weren't followed, humility was institutionalized into safety. Infections dropped by two-thirds. A resilient system was built not on brilliance, but on shared voice.

Corporate: The Ford Turnaround under Alan Mulally

Ford's leadership script used to be: "Hide bad news." Mulally rewrote it: "We can't fix what we don't face." Weekly Business Plan Reviews required leaders to color-code status honestly. Initially mocked, the ritual saved Ford from bankruptcy. Transparency became resilience.

Sports: The All Blacks Rugby Team

New Zealand's All Blacks embody resilience rituals. Leaders clean the locker room themselves ("sweeping the sheds"), modeling humility. They combine fierce performance with rituals of humility and gratitude, creating one of the most consistently dominant teams in sports history.

Humanitarian: Médecins Sans Frontières (MSF)

In war zones, MSF leaders practice daily debriefs where staff can voice emotional strain without stigma. These rituals prevent burnout and strengthen mission continuity under extreme stress.

Historical Anchors of Resilient Teams

- **The Shackleton Expedition (1914):** When trapped in Antarctic ice, Ernest Shackleton modeled humility by admitting limits and focusing on survival. His daily rituals of conversation and humor preserved morale. Every crew member survived.
- **The Apollo 13 Crisis (1970):** NASA engineers operated under the mantra "Failure is not an option." Yet humility was central: leaders admitted uncertainty, invited engineers at every level, and conducted relentless assumption testing. Emotional clarity under pressure brought the crew home.

Leader's Playbook: Building Resilient Teams

1. **Daily Check-In:** Begin meetings with one-word emotional states. Normalize emotion.
2. **Feedback Loops:** Adopt after-action reviews after major events. Leaders admit errors first.
3. **Voice Calibration:** Ask the lowest-status person first in discussions. This breaks hierarchy bias.
4. **Gratitude Ritual:** End Fridays with "one thing someone did that helped me this week."
5. **Red Team Rotation:** Rotate who challenges assumptions each week. Reward dissent that improves plans.
6. **Silence Audit:** Track who spoke least in meetings. Ask them privately what could invite their voice.
7. **Assumption Log:** Keep a visible record of key decisions and uncertainties. Review quarterly.

8. **Recovery Practices:** Model breaks, breathwork, and psychological detachment. Teams mirror what leaders normalize.
9. **Emotion Naming:** In tense moments, say what you see: "I sense frustration." This lowers threat perception.
10. **Celebration of Learning:** End projects by naming what mistakes taught—not just what successes proved.

Reflection Prompt #9

Think of your current team. Where do you see resilience—and where do you see fragility? Which ritual could you introduce this month to make humility, clarity, and voice part of the team's fabric?

Chapter Takeaway

Resilient teams aren't built by charismatic speeches or heroic gestures. They're built by leaders who model humility, regulate emotion, and create rituals of trust. Emotional clarity is not just an individual trait—it becomes a collective capacity when reinforced through daily practices.

The paradox is simple: when leaders stop performing invulnerability, teams grow invincible together.

Bridge to Chapter 10

If Chapter 9 explored resilience at the team level, Chapter 10 looks at decision-making at the leadership level. Because resilient teams need bold decisions—and **Chapter 10: The Courage to Decide** will show how humility doesn't weaken boldness, it fuels it. We'll explore how humble leaders make the hardest calls with clarity, courage, and conviction.

Chapter 10
The Courage to Decide—How Humility Fuels Bold Decisions

Every day, leaders face choices that affect not just projects and profits but people, cultures, and futures. The paradox is that humility—not bravado—is the key to bold decisions.

Decision-making is the crucible where leadership is truly tested. Some choices are small but cumulative—what meetings to hold, what priorities to fund. Others are seismic—launching a product, responding to a crisis, cutting or expanding. Most leaders believe bold decisions require unshakable confidence. The truth is more counterintuitive: the boldest decisions come from leaders humble enough to question their assumptions, seek dissenting views, and acknowledge what they don't know. Decision-making is the crucible of leadership. Every day, leaders face choices that affect not just projects and profits but people, cultures, and futures. Some decisions are small but cumulative—what meetings to hold, what priorities to fund. Others are seismic—when to launch a product, how to respond to a crisis, whether to cut or expand.

And yet, despite experience and intelligence, leaders often falter not because they lack data but because they are trapped by ego or fear. They hesitate, overanalyze, or cling to consensus in search of approval. Decision paralysis creeps in. Others swing the opposite way—making rash calls to prove authority or protect their image, only to reap unintended consequences.

The paradox is that humility—not bravado—is the key to bold decisions. Humble leaders don't shrink from responsibility. They step into it with clarity, courage, and consistency, focusing on long-term impact over short-term validation.

This chapter explores why humility is a decision-making superpower, how it rewires the brain away from ego-driven traps, and what frameworks can help leaders decide boldly when the stakes are high.

Decision Paralysis: When Ego and Fear Take the Wheel

Leaders are not strangers to indecision. Psychologist Roy Baumeister's foundational research on "ego depletion" demonstrated that repeated decision-making erodes willpower like a muscle tiring after exertion—with each choice consuming glucose in the brain's prefrontal cortex, the command center for complex reasoning, according to Substack Wikipedia. A 2023 study in Nature Neuroscience found that prolonged decision-making led to decreased activity in the prefrontal cortex, directly impairing executive function and decision-making ability (Monitask). When cognitive resources deplete, leaders fall into avoidance or impulsivity. Ego and fear intensify these traps.

Ego Trap: "If I'm wrong, I'll look weak." Leaders delay or obscure decisions to protect their image.

Fear Trap: "If I choose, I'll be blamed." Leaders push decisions upward or outward, waiting for safety that never arrives.

The Humility Advantage

The magnitude of decision fatigue's impact was starkly revealed in a landmark 2011 study published in the Proceedings of the National Academy of Sciences. Researchers analyzed over 1,100 parole decisions by experienced Israeli judges (with an average of 22.5 years of experience), and found that prisoners appearing early in a session received parole about 65% of the time. Still, this rate dropped gradually to nearly zero by the end of each session before a meal break, then abruptly returned to 65% after the break. PNAS. The implication is clear: when mental energy is low, decision-makers gravitate toward the default, status quo option—in this case, denial—regardless of case merits. Chief.

A 2018 study in Frontiers in Psychology found that fear of negative evaluation significantly predicted decision delay among managers. Similarly, research in Organizational Behavior and Human Decision Processes shows that leaders high in narcissism are more prone to overconfidence bias, ignoring disconfirming evidence. Both fear and ego distort judgment.

The real-world costs are substantial: A 2022 NHS report found that 42% of managerial errors in hospitals—such as misallocating resources or misdiagnosing priorities—stemmed from decision fatigue (Substack). Research by McKinsey found that executives wasting 30% of their time on low-impact decisions saw slower revenue growth, while a 2023 World Economic Forum study estimated that decision fatigue costs the global economy approximately $400 billion annually in lost productivity and poor decision outcomes (Monitask).

Case: Healthcare decision paralysis. In some hospitals, junior physicians hesitate to call a code because they fear being wrong. Delay costs lives. A 2015 BMJ Quality & Safety study revealed that hierarchical fear was a leading factor in delayed escalation during emergencies. Research in healthcare settings during COVID-19 found that decision fatigue not only reduced executive functioning but also increased susceptibility to cognitive heuristics—mental shortcuts that can bias decision-making and yield undesirable outcomes, with direct impacts on both healthcare workers' mental health and patient outcomes (PubMed Central). Where leaders normalized humility—"Better to call early and be wrong than late and be right"—response times improved dramatically.

Structured decision-making frameworks can rewire the brain to conserve cognitive energy. A 2021 Nature Human Behaviour study revealed that individuals using prioritization techniques reduced mental fatigue by 40%, freeing cognitive bandwidth for critical tasks (Substack). Humility cuts through ego and fear by reframing the act of deciding: from proving oneself to serving the mission.

The Neuroscience of Humble Decision-Making

Brain science helps explain why humility fosters better decisions.

- **Prefrontal Cortex (PFC):** Governs long-term planning, inhibition, and weighing trade-offs. Humility activates reflective PFC circuits, lowering impulsivity.

- **Amygdala:** Triggers fight-or-flight under threat. Ego-driven decision-making inflames amygdala reactivity ("protect image now"). Humility dampens this reactivity, enabling calm under stress.

- **Anterior Cingulate Cortex (ACC):** Detects errors and conflict. Humility allows leaders to use the ACC's signals as learning cues instead of shame triggers.

- **Default Mode Network (DMN):** Overactive DMN fuels rumination and self-referential worry. Humility quiets DMN chatter, creating space for clarity.

A 2014 study by Moran et al. showed that self-discrepancy (gap between actual and perceived self) triggers ACC distress and impaired executive function. Humility reduces this gap—leaders act from an accurate self-assessment, freeing mental bandwidth for decision quality.

Translation: Humility keeps the PFC online when ego or fear would otherwise hijack.

Understanding the neuroscience helps, but knowledge alone won't restore your depleted prefrontal cortex during a 12-hour decision marathon. Here are three research-backed practices that work with your brain's architecture, not against it:

1. **The 10-Minute Reset Walk**

The practice: Between major decisions or decision blocks, take a 10-minute walk—even if it's just pacing the hallway or doing laps around the parking lot.

The neuroscience: The 2020 Frontiers in Neuroscience study showed this restores executive function by 23% with effects lasting 2+ hours. Movement shifts blood flow and glucose allocation, activating restorative neural networks while giving the prefrontal cortex a break. It's not about cardio—it's about moving your body to reset your brain.

Universal application: Works in hospitals (walk the unit), offices (stairs or perimeter), military bases (anywhere there's ground). No equipment, no special setting needed.

2. The 5-Minute Complete Detachment Break

The practice: Set a timer for 5 minutes. Close your eyes or look out a window. Think about literally anything except work —a vacation memory, what you'll cook for dinner, your kid's soccer game. The key is full mental disengagement.

The neuroscience: Journal of Applied Psychology research found that 5-minute breaks with complete mental detachment restored decision capacity nearly as well as 30-minute breaks. Your prefrontal cortex needs to fully disengage to reallocate resources. Checking email or "light tasks" doesn't count—it keeps the decision circuits active.

Universal application: Can be done sitting at a desk, in a break room, in your car, or on a bench outside. Requires only 5 minutes and privacy in your own head.

3. Box Breathing Before Critical Decisions

The practice: Four counts in, four counts hold, four counts out, four counts hold. Repeat for 2-3 minutes before a major decision.

The neuroscience: Controlled breathing activates the parasympathetic nervous system, reducing cortisol and improving prefrontal cortex oxygenation. A 2018 study in

Frontiers in Psychology found that brief breathing exercises improved decision quality under stress by enhancing executive control and reducing emotional reactivity. It literally changes your brain state from reactive to deliberate.

Universal application: Can be done anywhere—before entering a meeting, in the moments before a difficult conversation, sitting in your office, or even standing in a hallway. Silent, invisible, takes under 3 minutes.

Choose one practice to implement this week. Master it for 30 days before adding another—transformation requires repetition, not collection.

Bold Decisions Are Values-Based, Not Validation-Based

Humble leaders distinguish between values and validation.

- **Validation-based decisions** seek approval: "Will this make me look good? Will the board like me? Will social media applaud?"

- **Values-based decisions** anchor in mission: "Does this align with our purpose? Does it serve people long-term? Does it reflect what we stand for?"

A study in Leadership Quarterly (Owens et al., 2015) showed that leaders who framed decisions around values rather than external praise earned greater long-term trust and organizational commitment. Short-term approval fluctuated, but long-term credibility deepened.

Example: Lincoln's Emancipation Proclamation. Abraham Lincoln knew emancipation risked political backlash, even within his own party. But his values—justice, unity, legacy—overrode validation. Historians argue that this values-based decision shifted the Civil War's moral center and reshaped the nation. Bold, humble decisions prioritize what endures.

Case Studies: Humility in High-Stakes Decisions

1. Sully on the Hudson (Aviation)

When both engines failed on US Airways Flight 1549, Captain Chesley "Sully" Sullenberger had seconds to decide. Instead of clinging to protocol or ego, he calmly assessed: no runway reachable, only the Hudson River. His humility showed in crediting the crew afterward—"We all did it together." The decision saved 155 lives. Neuroscientists later noted his ability to regulate amygdala reactivity and act from prefrontal clarity.

2. Tim Cook's Supply Chain Gamble (Tech)

When Tim Cook became CEO of Apple, one of his boldest decisions was continuing to invest heavily in China manufacturing despite political pressure to diversify. Rather than making the popular choice, he made the values-based one: Apple's commitment to quality required the precision manufacturing ecosystem that had taken decades to build. Critics called it risky; the decision was rooted in operational humility—admitting that reshoring couldn't yet match the quality standards Apple demanded. The gamble maintained Apple's product excellence while the company methodically built alternative supply chains.

3. The Ebola Response (Healthcare)

During the 2014 Ebola outbreak, MSF leaders faced impossible choices: deploy staff into high-risk zones or withdraw. Humility guided boldness—they acknowledged limits, shared data transparently, and empowered local staff. The decision to stay, rooted in mission rather than image, saved thousands.

4. Alan Mulally at Ford (Corporate)

Mulally inherited a culture of hiding bad news. In his first executive review, only one VP marked a program "red" (in trouble). Instead of punishing, Mulally applauded. That humble decision rewrote the culture—truth-telling became safe. Ford rebounded without a government bailout.

5. Dwight Eisenhower on D-Day (Military)

Before the invasion, Eisenhower drafted two notes: one accepting success, the other accepting blame if the operation failed. That act of humility freed him to decide boldly. History remembers his courage; few remember the note he was ready to read in failure.

Decision Frameworks for Humble Boldness

Humble leaders don't decide by gut alone. They use disciplined frameworks that tether judgment to values and reality.

1. The Values Filter

Ask four questions before deciding:

i. Does this align with our core purpose?
ii. Does it serve long-term outcomes over short-term optics?
iii. Does it treat people with dignity?
iv. Does this reflect who I want to become?

If yes → decide boldly.
If no → pause.

2. The Pre-Mortem

Psychologist Gary Klein's method: before implementing, imagine the decision failed. Ask, "What went wrong?" This humble exercise surfaces blind spots without shaming.

3. The 70% Rule

Jeff Bezos teaches: Act when you have 70% of the information. Waiting for 100% is ego-protection. Humility accepts risk, learns fast, and adjusts.

4. The Three Horizons

Adapted from scenario planning:

- **Horizon 1:** Immediate operational effect
- **Horizon 2:** Medium-term cultural impact
- **Horizon 3:** Long-term legacy

Humble leaders decide with all three in view, not just the next quarter.

5. The After-Action Loop

Every bold decision must be reviewed. Leaders admit what worked and what didn't. Humility makes feedback fuel, not failure.

The Risks of Arrogant or Fearful Decisions

- **Arrogant Decisions:** Made to prove competence, they ignore dissent and blind spots. Example: Challenger disaster (1986). Engineers' warnings about O-rings were dismissed by NASA leadership eager to validate capability. Tragedy followed.

- **Fearful Decisions:** Made to avoid blame, they stall progress. Example: Kodak executives hesitated to pivot to digital despite evidence, fearing loss of film profits. Ego and fear froze decision-making, and the company collapsed.

Both patterns show the same truth: ego kills boldness.

The Role of Psychological Safety in Team Decisions

Bold decisions are rarely solo acts. They emerge from collective intelligence. But teams contribute only when it feels safe.

- Google's Project Aristotle confirmed psychological safety as the strongest predictor of team performance.

- Healthcare research in BMJ Leader found that surgical teams with leaders who encouraged speaking up reported fewer complications.

- The Marine Corps after-action reviews institutionalize safety by encouraging leaders to name their own mistakes first, creating space for others.

Humble leaders make safety a precondition for decisive action.

Historical and Philosophical Anchors

Wisdom traditions have long tied humility to discernment:

- **Stoicism:** Epictetus taught, "First say to yourself what you would be, then do what you have to do." Stoic leaders are guided by values, not reputation.

- **Dhammapada:** "The wise are calm in thought and deed, beyond fear and fault." Quiet humility strengthens decision courage.

- **Biblical Anchor:** Proverbs 11:2: "When pride comes, then comes disgrace, but with humility comes wisdom." Across traditions, humility and wisdom are inseparable.

Leader's Playbook: Tools for Humble, Bold Decisions

Decision Journal: Record major decisions, reasoning, and expected outcomes. Review quarterly. This builds accuracy, not hindsight bias.

Dissent Invitation: Ask one person to argue against your decision. Reward their courage.

The Empty Chair: Leave a chair in the room to represent the absent stakeholder (patient, customer, future employee). Ask: "What would they say?"

Scenario Triad: For each decision, name the best-case, worst-case, and most-likely case. Humility acknowledges uncertainty.

Failure Letter: Write the "we failed" note before launching. This humbles the ego and strengthens accountability.

Feedback Forum: After decisions, debrief not just results but process. Ask: "What made this easier or harder to decide?"

Reflection Prompt #10

Think of a recent decision you delayed or avoided. What script drove it—ego ("I can't be wrong") or fear ("I can't be blamed")?

Now reframe: What would the values-based decision have been? What smallest bold move can you make this week from humility, not validation?

Chapter Takeaway

The world doesn't need leaders who decide faster or louder. It needs leaders who decide clearly, steadily, and humbly. Humility doesn't weaken boldness—it frees it.

- Ego seeks applause. Humility seeks alignment.

- Fear seeks safety. Humility seeks service.

- Arrogance clings to image. Humility clings to mission.

When leaders rewire decision-making from ego to humility, they unlock boldness that endures beyond the quarter, beyond their tenure, beyond themselves.

Bridge to Chapter 11

If Chapter 10 explored how humility fuels bold decisions in the moment, Chapter 11 widens the lens to eternity. Because the most important decisions aren't just about quarterly results —they're about legacy, faith, and eternal impact. Chapter 11: Faith, Identity, and Eternal Impact will show how leaders who anchor in something beyond themselves make decisions that reshape not just organizations, but generations.

Part IV: The Legacy of a Humble Leader

Chapter 11
Faith, Identity, and Eternal Impact
The measure of a leader is not taken in the noise of the moment, but in the echoes that remain when their voice has gone silent.

Titles fade, organizations change, fortunes vanish. What endures is the impact leaders have on people, on culture, and on the legacies they leave behind. This chapter explores the most profound dimension of leadership: how you define success when earthly measures no longer apply, and how faith —whether religious or philosophical—shapes the leader you become and the mark you leave on the world.

This chapter explores leadership through the lens of service and eternity. To lead with humility is to recognize that influence is not yours to hoard—it is yours to steward. To lead with eternity in mind is to recalibrate what matters, redefining success not as applause or advancement but as alignment with principles that outlast your lifetime.

How you define success matters profoundly. The metrics you choose—whether society's or your own—shape not only your leadership but your sense of self-worth, your vulnerability to imposter syndrome, and your capacity to lead with integrity. We'll return to this shortly.

The Hidden Architecture of Success

Before we examine leadership as service, we must confront a

foundational question that determines everything that follows: What does success actually mean to you?

This is not a rhetorical question. The answer shapes your daily decisions, your emotional resilience, and the legacy you leave. Most leaders inherit their definition of success rather than choose it. They absorb it from parents, from culture, from their industry, from Instagram feeds, and from LinkedIn titles. They measure themselves against metrics they never consciously adopted—revenue targets, promotions, followers, invitations, recognition.

The problem is not ambition. The problem is *borrowed* ambition—striving toward a finish line someone else drew, then wondering why crossing it feels hollow.

The Imposter Syndrome Connection

Research in the Journal of Behavioral Science (2019) found that imposter syndrome is most severe among high achievers who define success externally—those who measure their worth by others' approval or by comparison with peers. When success is defined as "being recognized," "never failing," or "staying ahead of colleagues," the internal experience becomes one of chronic inadequacy. No achievement ever feels sufficient because the goalpost is always moving, always external, always vulnerable to someone else's judgment.

Conversely, leaders who define success internally—through alignment with values, growth in character, or service to others—report significantly lower rates of imposter syndrome. Why? Because the metric is within their control. They can assess whether they acted with integrity today. They can measure whether they served someone well. They cannot control whether the market rewards them or whether a board appreciates their work, but they can control their faithfulness to principles.

This is not semantic. It is existential. Your definition of success determines whether you live in chronic anxiety or grounded confidence.

Society's Definitions vs. Eternal Definitions

Consider two leaders in the same organization:

Leader A defines success as: becoming VP within five years, earning a certain salary, being invited to speak at conferences, and having a prestigious title.

Leader B defines success as: developing others who surpass them, making decisions aligned with their values even when costly, and building something that serves people long after they're gone.

Both leaders work hard. Both are competent. But their internal experiences are radically different.

Leader A wakes up scanning for threats—who got promoted, who was quoted in the article, whose project got more resources. Their mood rises and falls with external validation. A passed-over promotion feels like failure. A critical email triggers existential doubt. They can't even give a genuine compliment to someone else for their good fortune because their identity is tethered to outcomes they do not fully control; they live in a state of perpetual vulnerability. They live in constant comparison.

Leader B wakes up asking different questions: Did I serve well yesterday? Am I aligned with my principles today? Who can I invest in this week? Because their definition of success is rooted in faithfulness and character, they experience setbacks as feedback, not as indictments of worth. A passed-over promotion may sting, but it does not shatter their sense of self. A critical email is information, not identity. They live in self-acceptance (focused on the moment rather than measuring against others).

This is what the Stoics meant when they distinguished between what is "up to us" and what is "not up to us." Marcus Aurelius wrote: "You have power over your mind—not outside events. Realize this, and you will find strength." External definitions of success hand power to outside events. Eternal definitions of success reclaim it.

Faith Traditions on Success

Scripture consistently redefines success in ways that subvert cultural norms.

In the Sermon on the Mount, Jesus declares the "successful" ones: the meek, the merciful, the pure in heart, the peacemakers (Matthew 5:3 9). Not the loudest, wealthiest, or most applauded—but those whose character reflects eternal values.

The Qur'an teaches: "But seek, through that which Allah has given you, the home of the Hereafter; and [yet], do not forget your share of the world" (Qur'an 28:77). Success is balanced—impact in this life and the next. It is not measured by accumulation but by stewardship and service.

In the Bhagavad Gita, Krishna tells Arjuna: "You have a right to perform your prescribed duties, but you are not entitled to the fruits of your actions" (2:47). Success, in this view, is found in dutiful action itself, not in outcomes. Leaders perform their roles with excellence, then release attachment to results.

The Talmud teaches: "Who is rich? One who is satisfied with his portion" (Pirkei Avot 4:1). Success is redefined as contentment and gratitude, not endless striving for more.

Across traditions, the pattern is clear: eternal success is measured by character, service, and alignment with transcendent values—not by comparison, accumulation, or applause.

Redefining Success: A Practical Exercise

Ask yourself these questions, and write your answers somewhere visible—on your desk, in your journal, in a note on your phone:

1. If I lost my title tomorrow, what would still make me feel successful?

2. When I am 80 years old, looking back on my leadership, what will I wish I had prioritized?

3. Whose opinion of my success actually matters to me—and why?

4. Am I measuring my worth by outcomes I control or by outcomes others control?

5. If no one knew about my work except me and God, would I still consider it successful?

These questions cut through cultural noise and force clarity. They expose borrowed metrics and surface what actually matters to you.

The Freedom of Internal Metrics

When you redefine success around internal metrics—faithfulness, character, service, growth—you liberate yourself from a prison most leaders never escape. You stop performing for an invisible audience. You stop contorting yourself to meet expectations you never agreed to. You stop collapsing under the weight of imposter syndrome, because you are no longer pretending to be something you are not. You are simply becoming who you were meant to be.

This does not mean abandoning external goals. You can still pursue promotions, build companies, and seek recognition. You can even seek financial wealth if you intend to do good things with it. But these become outcomes, not identities. They are results of your work, not measures of your worth. When you get them, you enjoy them. When you don't, you remain whole.

This shift—from externally defined success to eternally defined success—is the foundation of humble confidence. It is the prerequisite for every practice in this book. Because if you do not know what success actually means to you, every strategy becomes hollow, every achievement feels fragile, and every setback threatens to unravel you.

So define success now. Not as society defines it. Not as your industry defines it. Not as your insecurities whisper it. Define it as eternity would measure it.

Because how *you* define success determines everything else.

How to Make the Shift: From External to Internal Validation

Understanding the difference between external and internal success is one thing. Actually making the shift is another. Most leaders intellectually agree that internal metrics matter more, yet still find themselves checking LinkedIn obsessively, feeling deflated when someone else gets recognized, or measuring their worth by the size of their audience. The shift requires more than insight—it requires practice.

Here are seven concrete practices to retrain your nervous system away from external validation and toward internal integrity:

1. The Daily Integrity Audit

Each evening, before bed, answer three questions in a journal:

- Did I act with integrity today, even when no one was watching?
- Did I serve someone today in a way that mattered, even if unnoticed?
- Did I make at least one decision based on my values rather than on what would impress others?

This practice rewires your brain to seek internal affirmation rather than external applause. Over time, your dopamine system learns to reward character rather than comparison.

2. The 48-Hour Rule

When something good happens—a promotion, public recognition, a big win—allow yourself to enjoy it fully for 48 hours. Celebrate without guilt. But after 48 hours, consciously release it. Return to the question: "Who am I now that this moment has passed?" This prevents you from clinging to external validation as identity.

Conversely, when something disappointing happens—a rejection, criticism, a setback—give yourself 48 hours to feel it. Then release it with the same question: "Who am I beyond this outcome?"

3. Reframe the Question

Our brains are wired to ask: "What do they think of me?" This question hands your emotional state to external forces. Train yourself to ask a different question instead: "Did I honor my values in that moment?"

When you finish a presentation, resist the urge to scan the room for approval. Instead, ask: "Did I serve my audience well? Was I true to what I believe?" The shift is subtle but seismic.

4. Build an Eternal Scoreboard

Create a physical or digital "scoreboard" that tracks internal metrics, not external ones. This might include:

- Days I acted with integrity under pressure
- People I served without seeking credit
- Decisions I made aligned with my values, even when costly
- Moments, I chose humility over self-promotion

Review this weekly. Your brain needs tangible evidence that internal success is real, measurable, and worthy of attention.

Without this, external metrics will always feel more "real" because they're more visible.

5. Practice Anonymity

Intentionally do something generous, excellent, or helpful—and tell no one. Not your spouse, not your journal, not social media. Let it remain entirely between you and God (or your conscience, if you're secular). This practice is profoundly difficult for leaders accustomed to recognition, which is precisely why it's powerful. It severs the Pavlovian link between "I did something good" and "I need others to know."

Start small: pick up trash that no one saw you drop. Write an anonymous thank-you note. Fix a problem without taking credit. Each act trains you to find satisfaction in integrity itself, not in the applause that follows.

6. Curate Your Inputs

External validation becomes addictive partly because we marinate in environments that reinforce it. If you spend hours daily scrolling social media, reading industry news, or obsessing over competitors, your nervous system will prioritize external metrics—because that's what you're feeding it.

Audit your information diet:

- Unfollow accounts that trigger comparison or inadequacy
- Limit time on platforms engineered to harvest your attention
- Replace doomscrolling with reading scripture,

philosophy, classical, or wisdom literature that reinforces eternal values
- Spend time with people who affirm your character, not your achievements

Your attention is the architecture of your identity. Curate it ruthlessly.

7. The Eternal Perspective Reset

When you catch yourself spiraling into external validation—refreshing email for responses, checking metrics obsessively, feeling crushed by someone else's success—pause and do this:

Close your eyes. Take three deep breaths. Then ask: "Will this matter in 100 years?"

If the answer is no, release it. If the answer is yes (rare), ask the follow-up: "What would matter in 100 years is not the outcome, but how I respond. How do I want to respond with integrity?"

This practice doesn't eliminate ambition or the sting of disappointment. It simply relocates your emotional center from outcomes you don't control to responses you do.

The Shift Is Not a Switch—It's a Rhythm

Here's the hard truth: you will never fully eliminate the desire for external validation. It's neurologically hardwired. Even the most mature leaders feel a flutter of pleasure when praised or a sting of rejection when overlooked. The goal is not to become immune to external feedback—it's to ensure it doesn't define you. I remember hearing Dieter F. Uchtdorf describe some counsel he received from a more senior church leader, James E. Faust. To paraphrase, James told him, "Dieter, many people will be nice to you just because of the position you hold. Don't inhale it."

The shift from external to internal validation is not a one-time decision. It's a daily, sometimes hourly, recommitment. You will backslide. You will find yourself checking metrics you swore didn't matter. You will feel crushed by the criticism you claimed not to care about. This is normal. The question is not whether you'll slip—it's whether you'll return…who you let drive.

Return to the practices. Return to the questions. Return to the eternal scoreboard. Each return strengthens the neural pathway. Over time, the pulls of external validation weaken. Not because you've transcended being human, but because you've trained your soul to find satisfaction in something deeper.

The shift is possible. But it requires the humility to admit you're still learning—and the courage to keep practicing even when the world rewards the opposite.

Leadership as Service: The Oldest Truth, the Newest Research

The most enduring leaders have always framed leadership not as personal achievement but as service. Robert Greenleaf's seminal essay on servant leadership argued that the test of a leader is simple: Do those served grow as persons? True influence is measured not by the size of one's platform but by the flourishing of those under one's care. This vision echoes across scripture, philosophy, and science.

Latter-day Saint Tradition

Doctrine & Covenants 112:10 counsels: "Be thou humble; and the Lord thy God shall lead thee by the hand, and give thee answer to thy prayers." In this view, humility is not weakness but the condition for divine guidance. Leadership is service, but service flows first from submission to something greater than the self.

Buddhist Tradition

The Buddha framed leadership in terms of compassion and the relinquishing of ego. In the Dasa Raja Dharma (Ten Duties of a King), rulers are urged to practice generosity, morality, selflessness, and non-violence. Leadership, in Buddhist teaching, is an expression of the Noble Eightfold Path—particularly Right Intention (compassion rather than selfish desire) and Right Action. A true leader cultivates inner calm and outward compassion, seeing themselves as part of an interconnected web where service sustains harmony.

Stoic Philosophy

The Stoics argued that leadership was not about control but about aligning with nature and duty. Marcus Aurelius wrote in Meditations: "Waste no more time arguing about what a good man should be. Be one." For the Stoic leader, authority exists to serve the common good, not personal gain. Humility arises from recognizing that power is fleeting, but virtue—justice, temperance, wisdom, courage—is eternal. *Leadership without service is merely posturing; leadership with service becomes legacy.*

Modern Research

Harvard Business Review (2016) confirmed what these traditions intuited: leaders who frame their work as service report higher well-being and inspire more loyalty. Servant leadership correlates with lower turnover, greater engagement, and stronger resilience in teams. Service isn't just morally compelling—it's strategically effective.

Case example: Mother Teresa

Mother Teresa never sought a position or title, yet her influence spanned continents. Her identity was rooted in service, not recognition. She measured leadership not by scale but by faithfulness: "Not all of us can do great things. But we can do small things with great love." Her legacy exemplifies what Islamic scholars call barakah (spiritual blessing), what Buddhists call karuṇā (compassion), what Stoics call virtue in action, and what Christian scripture calls humility before God.

Across faiths and philosophies, the thread is clear: leadership divorced from service collapses into ego; leadership rooted in service becomes timeless.

Identity Anchored Beyond Achievement

Leaders who tie their identity only to achievement live in fragile cycles of striving. Their worth rises and falls with outcomes. When success is the sole measure, one failed project or one rejected proposal can feel like an existential crisis. By contrast, identity rooted in eternal perspective transcends this fragility. It creates steadiness that is unshaken by wins or losses because it draws from something deeper than performance.

Scriptural Anchors

In the Book of Mormon, the prophet Alma poses a piercing question: "Have ye walked, keeping yourselves blameless before God? Could ye say, if ye were called to die at this time, within yourselves, that ye have been sufficiently humble? ... Behold, are ye stripped of pride? I say unto you, if ye are not, ye are not prepared to meet God" (Alma 5:27–28). Here, humility is not weakness—it is preparation. Eternal identity is not found in the ego but in alignment with divine purpose.

The New Testament echoes this truth. Paul reminds the Galatians, "For am I now seeking the approval of man, or of God? Or am I trying to please man? If I were still trying to please man, I would not be a servant of Christ" (Galatians 1:10). The apostle reframes identity away from achievement or reputation, grounding it instead in service to God. Leadership, then, becomes less about proving worth and more about living faithfully.

Stoic Perspective

The Stoics offered a parallel in secular philosophy. Marcus Aurelius wrote in Meditations: "Ambition means tying your well-being to what other people say or do... Sanity means tying it to your own actions." For Stoics, true identity could not be dependent on the applause or judgment of others, nor on temporary outcomes. Anchoring self-worth in virtue—justice, courage, wisdom, temperance—created resilience. This resonates deeply with leaders today: the scoreboard may fluctuate, but character endures.

The Humility Advantage

Neuroscience of Identity

Modern research confirms what both scripture and Stoicism intuited. A 2019 study in *Frontiers in Psychology* found that individuals with a strong sense of transcendent identity—seeing themselves as part of something larger than themselves—reported higher resilience and lower stress under adversity. This kind of identity literally rewires the nervous system, creating patterns of steadiness rather than volatility. Leaders who see themselves as serving a greater purpose regulate stress more effectively and avoid burnout.

Corporate Parallel

Jim Collins, in Good to Great, identified "Level 5 Leaders" who embodied this paradoxical blend of fierce resolve and deep humility. Their leadership impact wasn't tied to personal ego. Instead, their identity was rooted in mission and contribution. Because of this, they built organizations that endured long after their tenure. Their leadership was about stewardship, not self-promotion.

The takeaway: Identity tethered to achievement alone will always be fragile. Identity tethered to eternal perspective—whether grounded in faith, virtue, or transcendent purpose—creates resilience, humility, and legacy.

Leading With Eternity in Mind

When leaders lift their vision from quarterly results to eternal impact, decision-making changes.

Short-term approval loses power. Eternal perspective asks: "Will this choice matter in 10 years? 50 years? 100 years?"

Fear of failure shrinks. Eternal perspective reframes failure as refinement, not identity.

Success redefined: Success becomes faithfulness, stewardship, and service, not applause or advancement.

Case: Abraham Lincoln. Critics mocked him mercilessly during the Civil War. But Lincoln's decisions were anchored in a vision of union and justice that outlived him. His assassination cut short his presidency, but his legacy reshaped a nation.

Case: Healthcare chaplains. Studies in *the Journal of Health Care Chaplaincy* show that chaplains anchor healthcare teams by keeping patient dignity and spiritual well-being central. Their influence endures not in reports but in how patients and families remember being treated. Eternal leadership reframes the metric.

The Paradox of Humility and Courage

Humility is not passivity; it is courage rightly directed. Leaders with eternal focus act boldly, but without arrogance.

Neuroscience: fMRI research on contemplative prayer (Newberg, 2016) shows reduced amygdala activation and increased prefrontal activity, allowing leaders to approach difficult decisions with calm clarity.

Faith Tradition: Jesus modeled this paradox—washing feet, forgiving enemies, yet resolutely moving toward His mission, which was His Father's mission. His leadership combined service with ultimate courage.

Modern example: Nelson Mandela emerged from 27 years in prison not with bitterness but with forgiveness. His humility redefined leadership in South Africa. His eternal perspective —justice and reconciliation—gave him the courage to risk political capital for peace.

Practices for Eternal Leadership

1. Journaling for Legacy

End each week by asking: "If my leadership were measured by one person's growth this week, who is it? What impact did I leave?"

2. Breath and Prayer Practice

Before major decisions, take five breaths and pray, aligning intent with service over ego. If you don't consider yourself religious or spiritual, find some quiet time to reflect.

3. Identity Anchoring Affirmation

"My worth is not in outcomes but in alignment with eternal purpose." Repeat in moments of doubt.

4. Mentorship with Generations in Mind

Shift from "How do I succeed?" to "How do I build successors who thrive after me?"

5. Eternal Time Horizon Exercise

Write decisions on two axes: impact now vs. impact in 100 years. Prioritize what survives both.

Historical Anchors of Eternal Leadership

George Washington: Twice relinquished power—after the Revolution and after his presidency. His humility modeled service over control, influencing democratic norms for centuries.

Florence Nightingale: Revolutionized nursing not for recognition but from faith-driven service. Her legacy persists in healthcare systems worldwide.

Dietrich Bonhoeffer: Opposed Nazi tyranny with humility and faith, writing from prison: "The ultimate test of a moral society is the kind of world it leaves to its children." His eternal lens fueled courage.

Faith at Work: Integrating Belief and Leadership

One of the most pressing questions leaders ask is, "How do I live my faith at work without forcing it on others?" Humility offers the bridge. Faith-driven leaders do not impose belief; they embody it through service, integrity, and compassion.

Research on Spiritual Leadership

A 2018 meta-analysis in the *Journal of Organizational Behavior* found that leaders who framed their role through spirituality—defined as meaning, purpose, and service—fostered higher organizational commitment and well-being in employees. These effects were strongest when paired with humility, because humility signaled openness rather than dogma.

Another study in Leadership Quarterly (Fry et al., 2021) showed that spiritual leadership predicted resilience and performance, particularly in healthcare systems under duress.

Leaders who led with purpose and values inspired greater perseverance among their teams.

Corporate example: Truett Cathy, Chick-fil-A. Cathy's Christian faith shaped his leadership, but not through preaching in the boardroom. Instead, he translated values into servant leadership, community investment, and genuine care for employees. His eternal perspective—service over profit—produced one of the most resilient, values-driven brands in America.

Healthcare example: Faith-based hospitals. Many Catholic and Protestant health systems explicitly integrate faith into mission—cura personalis (care of the whole person). Studies in *Health Care Management Review* confirm that these organizations sustain lower staff turnover when leaders emphasize service as a calling, not just a career. Eternal perspective fuels loyalty and trust.

Eternal Impact Beyond the Office

Eternal leadership is not confined to workplace metrics. Its true test is how people remember you once the position is gone.

Did you model dignity under pressure?

Did you serve the least visible people with the same respect as the most powerful?

Did you build successors who outshine you?

The paradox is that eternal impact often comes through small, hidden acts. In Matthew 25:40, Christ teaches: "Inasmuch as ye have done it unto one of the least of these my brethren, ye have done it unto me." Faith reframes even minor acts as eternal leadership moments.

Case: Desmond Tutu. Known worldwide for his fight against apartheid, Tutu's deepest legacy came from his pastoral presence. Survivors of violence recall his humility, his laughter, and his prayers more than his speeches. Eternal impact rests less on stagecraft and more on presence.

Expanded Playbook: Eternal Leadership in Daily Action

Service Audit: Each month, write how your leadership tangibly served someone—not just delivered outcomes.

Eternal Impact Review: Quarterly, ask: "What am I building that will outlast me?"

Micro-Acts of Service: Intentionally choose one "invisible" act daily— cover someone's parking meter, restock the break room without mentioning it, pause for someone overlooked.

Prayerful Discernment: Before major decisions, ask not only, "What works?" but, "What aligns with God's will and/or enduring values?"

Legacy Storytelling: Once a quarter, tell your team a story of someone whose humility shaped you. Stories carry values deeper than rules.

Eternity Journal: At month's end, write: "What did I do this month that will outlast me?" This reframes priorities.

The Legacy Ripple Effect

A study in the *Academy of Management Journal* (2020) found that leaders who communicated purpose beyond profit created "legacy motivation" in followers. Employees not only performed better but also adopted prosocial behaviors, even outside of work.

This aligns with scriptural teaching: "Let your light so shine before men, that they may see your good works, and glorify your Father which is in heaven" (Matthew 5:16). Legacy multiplies when service and faith guide leadership.

Reflection Prompt #11

If your leadership were remembered in one sentence by your team, what would it be today?

Now rewrite the sentence as you want it to be in 10, 50, 100 years or eternity. What shift in identity or practice would move you closer?

Chapter Takeaway

Eternal impact is not measured in the noise of markets or applause of peers but in the quiet testimonies of those who were lifted, healed, or strengthened by your presence. Faith, identity, and humility bind together into a leadership posture that serves not just this quarter, not just this decade, but eternity.

When leaders strip pride, they gain clarity. When they serve, they endure. When they lead with eternity in mind, they light paths that outlast them.

As Alma asked, "Have ye been sufficiently humble?" The answer determines not just influence in the room but impact in eternity.

Bridge to Chapter 12

If Chapter 11 examined eternal identity and legacy, Chapter 12 brings us back to the daily practices that sustain it. Because eternal impact isn't built in grand moments alone—it's built in the morning rituals, the breath before the meeting, the journal entry at night. Chapter 12: The Daily Practice of Humble Confidence will show how leaders anchor themselves day after day, staying rooted in humility amid influence, pressure, and growth.

The daily disciplines that make eternal impact possible.

The Humility Advantage

Download: Success Definition Exercise + Eternity Journal

Chapter 12
The Daily Practice of Humble Confidence

Confidence without humility turns brittle. Humility without confidence collapses into self-erasure. The leaders who endure are those who cultivate humble confidence—the capacity to walk into high-stakes moments grounded, steady, and open.

But how do you sustain this balance when the pressures mount, and old patterns resurface? Humble confidence isn't a destination you reach—it's a daily practice that requires intention, discipline, and grace. This chapter moves from theory to embodiment, offering the concrete rituals that keep you grounded in your authentic core even when everything around you is demanding you retreat back into your protective clay.

Humble confidence does not emerge from talent alone. It is not a personality trait you either have or don't. It is a practice, a discipline, a rhythm that must be renewed daily. Just as the body needs food and movement, the leader's soul needs ritual and recalibration.

This chapter explores the anchoring practices that build humble confidence day after day: stillness, breathwork, journaling, and gratitude. These are not luxuries; they are survival skills for leaders facing influence, pressure, and growth.

Why Daily Practice Matters

Neuroscience tells us that identity and behavior are not fixed —they are plastic, shaped by repetition. Long-term potentiation (LTP) strengthens neural pathways through consistent practice. Whatever you rehearse daily becomes your default.

- If you rehearse reactivity, you become reactive.
- If you rehearse presence, you become present.
- If you rehearse gratitude, you become generous.

A 2016 *Journal of Applied Psychology* study found that leaders who engaged in daily reflection rituals reported higher resilience, better decision-making, and greater team trust. Daily practices are not small—they are compounding investments in clarity and steadiness.

Anchoring Practices: The Morning Reset

1. Stillness - The Neuroscience of Silence: How Quiet Rewires the Brain

Silence is not merely stillness—it is a distinct neurological intervention with measurable effects on brain structure. A landmark 2015 study published in *Brain Structure & Function* by Duke University researchers found that two hours of silence per day led to the development of new brain cells in the hippocampus, the region critical for memory, learning, and emotional regulation. While other auditory stimuli (including Mozart piano music) showed short-term effects on cell proliferation, only silence remained associated with increased numbers of new neurons after seven days of exposure.

This phenomenon—called adult hippocampal neurogenesis—matters profoundly for leaders. The research team found that silence not only increased the raw number of precursor cells but also helped newly generated cells differentiate into functioning neurons and integrate into the brain's existing systems. Lead researcher Imke Kirste noted that "silence is really helping the newly generated cells to differentiate into neurons and integrate into the system," suggesting that these aren't dormant cells but active contributors to cognitive capacity. The implications are significant: conditions like dementia and depression have been linked to decreased neurogenesis in the hippocampus, raising the possibility that intentional silence could have therapeutic applications for cognitive resilience.

Beyond neurogenesis, silence also alters how the brain functions in the moment. In a 2021 study comparing work performance under different auditory conditions, participants working in silence experienced the least cognitive load and the lowest stress levels. The mechanism is straightforward: noise competes with our ability to perceive stimuli because we involuntarily process sound, diverting mental resources away from the task at hand. Silence removes this competition. A systematic review on silence and the autonomic nervous system found that "inner silence" enhances ventral vagus activity—associated with social engagement and calm—while reducing sympathetic nervous system activation and physiological stress.

Practical application: Begin your morning with intentional silence—not meditation with a mantra, not stillness with background sounds, but absolute auditory quiet. Set aside 10 minutes each morning in a space free from auditory input. No music. No podcasts. No ambient noise. Simply sit with the absence of sound. Notice the quality of your thoughts. Notice your body's response. The initial discomfort you may feel is your nervous system recalibrating away from chronic stimulation—a sign the practice is working. With repetition, silence becomes restorative rather than uncomfortable, creating a neural reset that prepares your hippocampus for the cognitive demands of leadership. The researchers predict that silence-activated cells should be usable for responding to cognitive challenges, as these new neurons survive the critical window during which survival-promoting forces are most effective. In other words, morning silence doesn't just calm you—it may literally be growing your brain's capacity to learn, remember, and lead.

2. Breathwork

Breath is the remote control of the nervous system. Leaders who master it carry portable calm into chaotic spaces.

Exercise: The Command State Primer

- **3-4** Rapid diaphragmatic (belly) breaths for 30 seconds
- Two deep inhales (completely inflate the lungs, hold briefly (3-4 seconds)
- Long pursed-lip exhale, hold briefly
- Repeat for 4–5 cycles

Processes (2016) shows that rituals reduce anxiety, improve performance consistency, and increase focus.

When leaders repeat grounding behaviors—breathwork before meetings, journaling at night—the brain associates ritual with readiness. Confidence becomes less about outcome and more about preparation.

Historical Anchors: Humble Confidence Across Time

- **Jesus Christ:** Modeled humble confidence—washing feet one moment, confronting hypocrisy the next. His presence was steady because His identity was anchored in eternal purpose.

- **Mahatma Gandhi:** Practiced daily prayer and fasting to keep ego in check. His confidence flowed from discipline, not dominance.

- **Epictetus (Stoic):** Reminded students to distinguish between what is in their control and what is not. Humble confidence is clarity about limits and responsibilities.

Leader's Playbook: Daily Practice of Humble Confidence

1. **Morning Stillness (10 minutes):** Begin with silence before the noise.

Staying Rooted Amid Pressure and Growth

The higher the leaders rise, the more tempting it becomes to cling to an image. Influence magnifies ego risk. Growth multiplies pressure.

Case study: Jensen Huang at Nvidia

Huang entered as CEO of a graphics chip company and transformed it into an AI powerhouse. Through decades of pressure—near-bankruptcy moments, competitive threats, and technological pivots—he maintained daily practices of learning and curiosity. His ritual? Starting each day by reading technical papers and asking engineers to teach him. His humility about what he didn't know turned pressure into innovation rather than defensiveness.

Healthcare example: Intensive Care Unit (ICU) leaders

ICU directors face constant pressure—life-and-death stakes, staff shortages, complex decisions. Those who practiced daily centering (mindfulness, gratitude rounds) reported lower burnout and higher team cohesion (*BMJ Leader*, 2021).

Athletics example: Michael Phelps

Before races, Phelps rehearsed visualization and breathwork daily. He attributed his calm to ritual, not talent. His practice-based confidence allowed him to recover from setbacks and dominate under pressure.

The Science of Ritual Under Pressure

Rituals are not superstition; they are neurological stabilizers. Research in *Organizational Behavior and Human Decision*

4. Gratitude

Gratitude is not soft—it's neurochemical. Research shows that gratitude practices increase dopamine and serotonin levels, stabilizing mood and expanding perspective.

Study: A 2017 *Personality and Individual Differences* study found that leaders who practiced daily gratitude were rated as more approachable, trustworthy, and resilient.

Practical move: End each day by writing three specific gratitudes. Shift from generic ("I'm grateful for my team") to precise ("I'm grateful Sarah challenged my assumption and improved our decision"). Precision makes gratitude credible.

Recalibrating Identity Daily

Leadership pressures can distort identity. Success tempts arrogance. Failure tempts despair. Growth brings new scrutiny. Without daily recalibration, leaders drift into either overconfidence or self-erasure.

The Mirror Ritual

Ask each morning:

- Who am I when I am most grounded?
- What do I want to embody today?

This ritual keeps identity centered in values, not performance.

Faith anchor: In Doctrine & Covenants 112:10, leaders are reminded: *"Be thou humble; and the Lord thy God shall lead thee by the hand."* Daily humility aligns identity with divine guidance, recalibrating purpose.

This routine lowers cortisol, increases heart rate variability (HRV), and re-engages prefrontal clarity. Research in *Frontiers in Psychology* confirms breathwork as one of the fastest, most reliable ways to regulate the state.

Case example: Surgeons who practiced paced breathing before procedures showed lower stress and fewer errors (*Journal of the American College of Surgeons*, 2018).

3. Journaling

Writing externalizes thought and builds metacognition. Leaders who journal don't just process events—they shape identity.

Exercise: The Two-Column Journal

- **Left column:** Inner critic voice
- **Right column:** Grounded truth reframe

This exercise, rooted in cognitive behavioral therapy (CBT) techniques, reduces rumination and builds confidence.

Corporate example: Howard Schultz, former CEO of Starbucks, journaled his doubts and fears. By naming them on paper, he reframed them into commitments. His journals became blueprints of resilience.

Military example: Marine Corps officers are encouraged to practice after-action journaling to separate fact from feeling, building humility and accuracy in identity.

2. **Breathwork Reset:** Use the Command State Primer before high-stakes moments.
3. **Two-Column Journal:** Counter the critic daily.
4. **Daily Gratitude List:** Name three precise gratitudes before sleep.
5. **Mirror Ritual:** Each morning, state: "Today I will embody humility and confidence."
6. **Voice Calibration:** In one meeting daily, speak with clarity—not to dominate, but to contribute.
7. **Identity Anchor Card:** Carry a pocket card with a daily affirmation. For example: "My worth is not in outcomes but in alignment with values."
8. **Weekly Reflection Sabbath (whatever day you choose):** One day or half-day unplugged for rest, review, and recalibration.
9. **Mentor Touchpoint:** Weekly check-in with someone who reminds you of values, not status.
10. **Service Audit:** Each week, name one invisible act of service you performed.

Reflection Prompt #12

What ritual currently anchors you when pressure rises? Is it strong enough to carry you through growth?

Write one new daily practice you will adopt this week. Pair it with a morning or evening trigger (breath before morning beverage, journal before bed). Consistency rewires confidence.

Chapter Takeaway

Humble confidence is not about projecting invulnerability. It is about cultivating daily rhythms that keep you grounded in values, steady under pressure, and open to others.

- Stillness calms
- Breath steadies
- Journaling reframes
- Gratitude expands

The world does not need louder leaders. It needs steadier ones—leaders who rise each morning not to perform but to serve, who carry calm certainty into chaos, who anchor in humility even as influence grows.

Bridge to Conclusion

You've journeyed through twelve chapters exploring the paradox of humble leadership. You've learned that the armor protecting you was also weighing you down. You've discovered that true humility isn't weakness—it's the neurological, relational, and spiritual foundation of lasting influence.

Now, one final truth remains: **You were never a fraud. You were becoming a leader.**

The Conclusion will bring us full circle—back to the Golden Buddha, back to the clay and the gold, back to the central revelation that has guided this entire journey: the disguise you wore for protection has served its purpose. It's time to let the gold shine through.

CONCLUSION
You Were Never a Fraud—
You Were Becoming a Leader

The world is changed by those who lead from love, not ego.

In 1957, a group of monks at Wat Traimit Temple in Bangkok prepared to relocate a large Buddha statue. The image was over ten feet tall, weighed several tons, and—by all appearances—was made of plain stucco. During the move, the rigging slipped, and the statue fell, cracking the surface. A glint flashed from the fracture.

We began this book with that story. Now, twelve chapters later, we return to it—not as metaphor alone, but as lived reality.

You are the Golden Buddha. (I'm sensitive, self-aware, and maybe even humble enough to admit I get a little teary writing that... *YOU ARE THE GOLDEN BUDDHA!!*)

The clay you've carried—the armor of achievement, the mask of certainty, the performance of invulnerability—was never your true identity. It was protection. And for a season, it served you well. It got you through chaos, through hierarchies that punished weakness, through environments where doubt felt like death.

But you've outgrown the disguise.

The weight you've been carrying isn't gold—it's clay. And every time you lead from fear instead of presence, every time you silence your voice to avoid exposure, every time you chase validation instead of values, you're bowing to the disguise instead of revealing the truth beneath.

This book has been about the crack. The fracture that lets the light through.

What You've Learned

Let's trace the journey you've taken:

Part I: The Inner War

You learned that imposter syndrome isn't a character flaw—it's a predictable response to high-stakes environments. You discovered that the mask you wear to protect yourself is the same mask that's suffocating your potential. You recognized that false humility—shrinking to avoid exposure—is just fear in a different costume. And you met the inner critic, that voice that's been running scripts written decades ago by people who are no longer in the room.

Part II: Reclaiming Your Power

You discovered that humility isn't weakness—it's a measurable brain state that activates empathy, trust, and long-term thinking. You learned how to rewrite the limiting scripts you've been running, replacing "I don't belong" with "I earned this" and "Don't speak up" with "My voice serves the mission." You gained tools: breathwork, journaling, visualization, identity-based affirmations—not as soft skills, but as neurological rewiring.

Part III: Leadership from the Center

You learned to lead from clarity, courage, and consistency—anchoring in wisdom instead of wounds. You discovered that quiet confidence isn't about volume or charisma; it's about being present enough to speak clearly, humble enough to invite input, and steady enough to receive feedback without flinching. You saw how resilient teams aren't built by heroic individuals but by leaders who model humility, regulate emotion, and create rituals of trust.

Part IV: The Legacy of a Humble Leader

You explored how humility fuels bold decisions—not by making you hesitant, but by freeing you from the need to protect your image. You confronted the foundational question of how you define success, distinguishing between borrowed metrics that create chronic anxiety and eternal definitions that anchor you in character, service, and faithfulness. You examined leadership through the lens of eternity, discovering that the most important decisions aren't about quarterly results but about legacy, faith, and impact that outlasts you. You learned practical ways to shift from external validation to internal integrity—through daily audits, the 48-hour rule, and building an eternal scoreboard. And you discovered that humble confidence isn't a destination—it's a daily practice, renewed each morning through stillness, silence, breath, gratitude, and recalibration.

The Central Paradox

Throughout this journey, one paradox has echoed:

When you stop needing to prove your worth, you become unstoppable.

When you let go of needing the credit, you gain the influence.

When you lead from humility, you lead with power.

This isn't motivational rhetoric. It's neuroscience. It's organizational research. It's the wisdom of the Stoics, the teaching of Christ, the insight of Buddhist masters, and the findings of leadership scholars over the decades.

Humility doesn't erase your voice—it amplifies it.

Humility doesn't diminish your authority—it grounds it.

Humility doesn't make you weak—it makes you unshakable.

You Were Never a Fraud

Let's name the lie you've carried for too long:

"I'm not really good enough. Any day now, they'll find out."

The Humility Advantage

That voice has cost you sleep, relationships, opportunities, and peace. It's made you overwork, over-prepare, and over-apologize. It's kept you silent when you should have spoken, small when you should have stepped forward, performing when you should have been present.

But here's the truth the clay has been hiding:

You were never a fraud. You were becoming.

Every doubt you've wrestled with? That's not evidence of inadequacy—it's evidence of growth. The gap between your external success and internal confidence doesn't prove that you don't belong. It's proof that you're stretching into a new capacity faster than your identity can integrate it.

The inner critic that whispers "You're not ready"? It's not the truth. It's an old alarm system running on outdated programming, trying to protect you from threats that no longer exist.

The imposter syndrome you've battled? It's not a flaw. It's the growing pains of a leader who cares deeply, who leads well, and who is committed to something bigger than ego.

Choosing Humility as a Path to Influence

You stand at a choice point.

You can continue wearing the clay—performing confidence you don't feel, protecting an image that exhausts you, leading from fear instead of presence. The disguise will keep you safe. But it will also keep you small.

Or you can choose the fracture. The crack. The honest admission that you don't have all the answers, that you need your team's voice, that you're learning as you lead.

That choice feels vulnerable. It feels like exposure.

But here's what the research shows, what the case studies prove, what the wisdom traditions have taught for millennia:

The moment you stop performing invulnerability, you unlock true influence.

- When Tim Cook said, "The best decision I can make, not the decision that makes me look good," he anchored Apple's culture in mission over image.

- When Jensen Huang said, "I don't know—help me understand," he created a culture where truth-telling became Nvidia's competitive advantage.

- When Marine Corps leaders admit their mistakes first in after-action reviews, they turn fear into safety and silence into learning.

- When healthcare leaders pause three seconds before responding to criticism, they regulate not just their own nervous system but their team's.

Humility is not the path to insignificance. It's the path to lasting influence.

The World Changed by Humble Leaders

The world doesn't need more arrogant leaders who dominate rooms.

It doesn't need more self-erasing leaders who shrink from responsibility.

It needs you.

The real you. Not the mask. Not the performance. Not the over-functioning, over-proving, over-compensating version.

The you who leads from grounded confidence, who speaks from clarity instead of fear, who builds teams where truth is cheap to say and safety is woven into every ritual.

The world is changed by leaders who:

- Admit uncertainty before it becomes a crisis
- Invite dissent before it becomes a disaster
- Credit others before taking the stage
- Serve quietly before leading loudly

The world is changed by those who lead from love, not ego.

And that leader is you—once you stop performing and start revealing.

Your Next Step

This book ends, but your work continues.

You have tools now:

- The two-column journal to reframe the criticism
- The breath reset to the regulating state
- The clarity script to speak with authority and openness
- The after-action review to normalize learning
- The identity anchor to stay centered amid pressure

You have frameworks:

- The values filter for bold decisions
- The three horizons for long-term thinking
- The pre-mortem to surface blind spots
- The 70% rule to act without perfect certainty

You have rituals:

- Morning stillness to anchor before the noise
- Check-in circles to normalize emotion
- Gratitude rounds to build trust
- Blameless postmortems to turn error into learning

But tools, frameworks, and rituals mean nothing without commitment.

So here's your choice:

Will you keep bowing to the clay? Or will you crack the disguise and let the gold shine?

Afterword

If I could reduce this entire book to three simple rules, they would be:

1. Love and be kind to yourself and others.
2. Love and be kind to yourself and others.
3. Love and be kind to yourself and others.

APPENDIX A: Complete Exercise Index

What follows is a comprehensive list of all the exercises in this book. Read through this, determine what you need to do first as an individual, and then pick another to run meetings. Chip away at the list bit by bit, working on one or a few at a time until you're ready to add more.

INDIVIDUAL EXERCISES & PRACTICES

SELF-ASSESSMENT & REFLECTION

Chapter 1: Uncovering the Gold Within

Telltale Behaviors Self-Check (p. 18)

- Default to certainty in meetings, even when only 60% sure
- Keep "quick wins" for yourself and delegate messy work reluctantly
- Delay hard feedback because you fear backlash
- Hear dissent as disrespect instead of data

Reflection Prompt #1: Plaster vs. Gold (p. 30)

- Where are you operating from, plaster instead of gold?
- Name the behavior in a sentence that a direct report would recognize
- Decide the smallest, most public crack you're willing to make this week

Chapter 2: The Cost of the Mask

Leader's Health Red Flags Audit (p. 43)

- Chronic exhaustion, stress-related illness, withdrawal
- Silence in meetings, avoidance of stretch work, over-control
- Green dashboards hiding red reality, high turnover, low error reporting

Reflection Prompt #2: Earning Your Right (p. 43)

- Where are you still trying to earn your right to be here?
- Name the specific behavior, not the feeling
- Write one sentence you'll say in your next meeting to crack the mask

Chapter 3: The False Self

Reflection Prompt #3: False Humility Check (p. 54)

- Where do you practice "false humility"—minimizing yourself to avoid exposure?
- Write one sentence you could say that balances strength and openness
- Example: "I'm confident this approach is sound. The risk I want us to examine is..."

Chapter 4: Unmasking the Inner Critic

Reflection Prompt #4: Naming the Distortion (p. 71)

Think of a recent moment when your inner critic spoke loudest

Write down the exact words it used

Label the distortion (all-or-nothing, catastrophizing, mind reading, etc.)

Replace with one grounded truth you can carry forward

DAILY PRACTICES & RITUALS

Chapter 5: Humility Rewired

The Pause-and-Presence Drill (p. 83)

- Before responding in high-stakes moments: exhale slowly
- Ask: "What outcome matters most—my image or the mission?"
- Then respond

Gratitude Reframe (p. 83)

- When receiving credit, replace deflection ("It was nothing")
- With shared ownership: "Thank you—I'm proud of what the team accomplished"

Perspective Switch (p. 83)

- Intentionally imagine what the other person is experiencing in a meeting
- Primes mirror neurons for empathy

Structured Pauses (p. 83)

- Pause for three seconds before responding to difficult input
- Interrupts reactivity and signals humility

The "Two Admits" Rule (p. 84)

- In any contentious discussion, admit two things you learned or got wrong
- Do this before defending your view

The "Ask-Then-Answer" Turn (p. 84)

- Before presenting a solution, ask: "What's the core constraint as you see it?"
- Surface hidden data and increase buy-in

Daily Self-Check (p. 85)

- At day's end, ask: Where did I react to protect ego instead of serve mission?

Trust Audit (p. 85)

- Identify who on your team hesitates to speak the truth
- What would lower their cortisol and raise their oxytocin?

Perspective Practice (p. 86)

- In one meeting a week, say: "Here's what I don't know and where I need your input"

Learning Loop (p. 86)

- Model curiosity by asking one genuine, non-rhetorical question in every conversation

Reflection Prompt #5: Reactivity Reframe (p. 88)

- Think back to your last moment of reactivity
- What triggered it—ego, fear, image protection?
- Write one sentence reframing how you could have responded from humility

Chapter 6: Rewriting the Script

The "Two-Column Journal" (p. 97)

- Column A: Write the critic's script ("I'm always behind," "I'll fail if I delegate")
- Column B: Write the grounded reframe ("I manage priorities; I can delegate without losing control")

The Command State Breath (p. 98)

- Double inhale through the nose
- Hold for two seconds
- Long exhale through pursed lips
- Repeat 4–5 times

Identity-Based Affirmations (p. 98)

- Replace limiting statements ("I'm not confident")
- With identity statements ("I am a leader who practices calm presence")

The Leadership Rehearsal (Focused Visualization) (p. 100)

- Close your eyes and visualize the upcoming high-stakes moment
- Imagine yourself entering calm, breathing evenly, naming uncertainty, inviting input
- Repeat daily for one week

Script Audit (Weekly) (p. 104)

- Write down one recurring self-limiting phrase
- Test it with evidence
- Replace with a grounded truth

Breath-Anchor Ritual (p. 105)

- Before key meetings, practice three cycles of double inhale/long exhale
- Let breath be the bridge to presence

Identity Affirmation Card (p. 105)

- Write one identity-based statement aligned with values
- Example: "I am a leader who grows by listening"
- Keep it visible

Visualization Rehearsal (p. 105)

- Spend five minutes daily picturing yourself leading from humility and presence

Voice Calibration (p. 105)

- In one meeting per week, speak early—not to dominate, but to break the silence script

Celebration Journal (p. 106)

- End each day by writing one example of when you showed calm certainty
- Repetition encodes identity

Reflection Prompt #6: Script Rewrite (p. 107)

- Write the current script that holds you back

- Be brutally honest: what words echo before you speak, decide, or lead?
- Rewrite it: Draft the script you want to carry—rooted in calm certainty and grounded worth
- Say it aloud once a day this week

Chapter 7: Centered Leadership

The Centering Breath (p. 115)

- Inhale for four counts
- Hold for four counts
- Exhale for six counts
- Hold for two counts
- Repeat three times before a high-stakes interaction

The "Wisdom Over Wounds" Journal (p. 116)

- Write one wound-driven script that echoes in your leadership
- Example: "Don't let anyone see weakness"
- Rewrite it as wisdom: "Strength is making space for others' voices"
- Repeat weekly

The Non-Reactivity Cue (p. 116)

- Pick a small anchor (touching your pen, taking a sip of water)
- Each time you feel triggered, use the cue to pause before responding
- Over time, the pause becomes a habit

The Humility Advantage

Detachment Practice (p. 116)

- At the end of the day, ask: "Where did I react to praise or blame today?"
- Note it without judgment
- With repetition, identity shifts from performance to presence

Daily Centering (p. 117)

- Begin the day with breath or meditation practice to anchor before emails and meetings

Wisdom Journaling (p. 118)

- Reframe one wound-driven script weekly into a wisdom statement

Consistency Audit (p. 118)

- Ask colleagues privately: "Do I show up the same in pressure as in calm?"
- Track patterns

Non-Attachment Check (p. 119)

- Notice when praise inflates you, or criticism crushes you
- Name it. Re-anchor in values

Reflection Prompt #7: Triggered by Praise or Blame (p. 120)

- Think of a recent moment when you were triggered by either praise or blame
- Write the script your wound wanted to run
- Write the wiser script you wish to embody
- Commit to practicing that script in your next leadership moment

Chapter 8: Quiet Confidence

The Clarity Script (p. 132)

Before a meeting, write three short sentences:

- What I know
- What I don't know
- What I recommend

Deliver these first

The Curiosity Cue (p. 132)

- End each statement with one open-ended question
- Example: "Here's my view. What am I missing?"

Feedback Reframe (p. 132)

- When criticized, mentally replace "attack" with "data"
- Ask: "What signal can I use from this?"

The Humility Advantage

Body Scan Reset (p. 132)

- Before entering a room, pause
- Drop shoulders, unclench jaw, breathe evenly
- Signals steadiness

Micro-Gratitude Practice (p. 132)

- When someone challenges you, thank them aloud: "That's helpful—thank you"
- Gratitude disarms defensiveness and models strength

Posture Check-In (p. 133)

- Ask a trusted colleague: "Do I look defensive when challenged?"
- Awareness precedes change

Presence Audit (p. 134)

- Ask a trusted peer: Do I shrink in silence or posture with arrogance? Where do you see it?

Voice Calibration (p. 134)

- In your next meeting, aim for a measured tone, short sentences, and one open invitation for feedback

Feedback Ritual (p. 135)

- When criticized, write down three possible truths in the comment before reacting

Posture Practice (p. 135)

- Video yourself in a meeting
- Review for signals of defensiveness (crossed arms, clenched jaw) vs. openness (eye contact, relaxed shoulders)

Daily Detachment (p. 135)

- At day's end, ask: "Did I act from ego today or from mission?"
- Re-anchor tomorrow

Confidence Journal (p. 135)

- Each night, write one moment when you spoke with clarity and one when you stayed silent
- Track patterns

Reflection Prompt #8: Speaking with Quiet Confidence (p. 135)

- Think of a time you stayed silent when you had something valuable to add
- What script held you back?
- Imagine yourself speaking with quiet confidence—what would you have said?
- Write it down. Practice saying it aloud

DECISION-MAKING TOOLS

Chapter 6: Rewriting the Script

The 5-Minute Breath Reset (p. 97)

- Before deciding, pause for three cycles of deep breath
- Lower cortisol, engage prefrontal clarity

Chapter 10: The Courage to Decide

The Values Filter (p. 157)

Ask three questions before deciding:

- Does this align with our core purpose?
- Does it serve long-term outcomes over short-term optics?
- Does it treat people with dignity?

If yes → decide boldly. If no → pause

The Pre-Mortem (p. 158)

- Before implementing, imagine the decision failed
- Ask: "What went wrong?"
- Surfaces blind spots without shaming

The 70% Rule (p. 158)

- Act when you have 70% of the information
- Waiting for 100% is ego-protection

The Three Horizons (p. 158)

Evaluate decisions on three axes:

- Horizon 1: Immediate operational effect
- Horizon 2: Medium-term cultural impact
- Horizon 3: Long-term legacy

Decision Journal (p. 160)

- Record major decisions, reasoning, and expected outcomes
- Review quarterly to build accuracy, not hindsight bias

Scenario Triad (p. 161)

For each decision, name:

- Best-case
- Worst-case
- Most likely case

Humility acknowledges uncertainty

Failure Letter (p. 161)

- Write the "we failed" note before launching

- Humbles the ego and strengthens accountability

Reflection Prompt #10: Values-Based Decision (p. 161)

- Think of a recent decision you delayed or avoided
- What script drove it—ego ("I can't be wrong") or fear ("I can't be blamed")?
- Reframe: What would the values-based decision have been?
- What smallest bold move can you make this week from humility, not validation?

LEGACY & PURPOSE PRACTICES

Chapter 11: Faith, Identity, and Eternal Impact
SUCCESS DEFINITION & INTERNAL VALIDATION

Redefining Success: A Practical Exercise (p. 169)

Ask yourself these questions and write your answers somewhere visible:

- If I lost my title tomorrow, what would still make me feel successful?
- When I am 80 years old, looking back on my leadership, what will I wish I had prioritized?
- Whose opinion of my success actually matters to me —and why?

- Am I measuring my worth by outcomes I control or by outcomes others control?
- If no one knew about my work except me and God, would I still consider it successful?

The Daily Integrity Audit (p. 171)

Each evening, before bed, answer three questions in a journal:

- Did I act with integrity today, even when no one was watching?
- Did I serve someone today in a way that mattered, even if unnoticed?
- Did I make at least one decision based on my values rather than on what would impress others?

The 48-Hour Rule (p. 171)

- When something good happens—allow yourself to enjoy it fully for 48 hours, then consciously release it
- Ask: "Who am I now that this moment has passed?"
- When something disappointing happens—give yourself 48 hours to feel it, then release with the same question

Reframe the Question (p. 172)

- When you catch yourself asking, "What do they think of me?"
- Replace with "Did I honor my values in that moment?"

The Humility Advantage

Build an Eternal Scoreboard (p. 172)

Create a physical or digital scoreboard that tracks internal metrics:

- Days I acted with integrity under pressure
- People I served without seeking credit
- Decisions I made aligned with my values, even when costly
- Moments when I chose humility over self-promotion

Review weekly

Practice Anonymity (p. 173)

- Intentionally do something generous, excellent, or helpful—and tell no one
- Not your spouse, not your journal, not social media
- Start small: Stay late to finish a colleague's task anonymously, leave an encouraging note where only one person will find it, and fix a problem without taking credit.

Curate Your Inputs (p. 173)

Audit your information diet:

- Unfollow accounts that trigger comparison or inadequacy
- Limit time on platforms designed to monetize your attention
- Replace doomscrolling with reading scripture, philosophy, or wisdom literature

- Spend time with people who affirm your character, not your achievements

The Eternal Perspective Reset (p. 174)

- Close your eyes, take three deep breaths
- Ask: "Will this matter in 100 years?"
- If no → release it
- If yes → ask: "What would matter is not the outcome, but how I respond. How do I want to respond with integrity?"

ETERNAL LEADERSHIP PRACTICES

Journaling for Legacy (p. 181)

- End each week by asking: "If my leadership were measured by one person's growth this week, who is it? What impact did I leave?"

Breath and Prayer Practice (p. 181)

- Before major decisions, take five breaths and pray
- Align intent with service over ego

Identity Anchoring Affirmation (p. 181)

- "My worth is not in outcomes but in alignment with eternal purpose"
- Repeat in moments of doubt

The Humility Advantage

Eternal Time Horizon Exercise (p. 181)

- Write decisions on two axes: impact now vs. impact in 100 years
- Prioritize what survives both

Service Audit (p. 184)

- Each month, write how your leadership tangibly served someone—not just delivered outcomes

Eternal Impact Review (p. 184)

- Quarterly, ask: "What am I building that will outlast me?"

Micro-Acts of Service (p. 184)

- Intentionally choose one "invisible" act daily
- Pick up trash, write a thank-you note, pause for someone overlooked

Prayerful Discernment (p. 184)

- Before major decisions, ask not only "What works?" but "What aligns with God's will and enduring values?"

Eternity Journal (p. 184)

- At month's end, write: "What did I do this month that will outlast me?"

- Reframes priorities

Reflection Prompt #11: Leadership Legacy (p. 185)

- If your leadership were remembered in one sentence by your team, what would it be today?
- Rewrite the sentence as you want it to be in eternity
- What shift in identity or practice would move you closer?

COMPLETE DAILY PRACTICE SYSTEM

Chapter 12: The Daily Practice of Humble Confidence

Morning Stillness (10 minutes) (p. 196)

- Begin with silence before the noise
- Eyes open, no agenda
- Simply notice breath, body, and thought

The Command State Primer (Breathwork) (p. 197)

- Rapid diaphragmatic breaths for 30 seconds
- Two deep inhales, hold briefly
- Long pursed-lip exhale, hold briefly
- Repeat for 4–5 cycles

The Humility Advantage

Two-Column Journal (p. 197)

- Left column: Inner critic voice
- Right column: Grounded truth reframe

Daily Gratitude List (p. 197)

- Name three precise gratitudes before sleep
- Shift from generic to specific

The Mirror Ritual (p. 197)

- Who am I when I am most grounded?
- What do I want to embody today?

Identity Anchor Card (p. 197)

- Carry a pocket card: "My worth is not in outcomes but in alignment with values"

Weekly Reflection Sabbath (p. 197)

- One day or half-day unplugged for rest, review, and recalibration

Mentor Touchpoint (p. 197)

- Weekly check-in with someone who reminds you of values, not status

Service Audit (p. 197)

- Each week, name one invisible act of service you performed

Reflection Prompt #12: Ritual Anchor (p. 197)

- What ritual currently anchors you when pressure rises?
- Is it strong enough to carry you through growth?
- Write one new daily practice you will adopt this week
- Pair it with a morning or evening trigger

TEAM & GROUP EXERCISES

TEAM MEETINGS & RITUALS

Chapter 2: The Cost of the Mask

10-Minute Weekly Practice (p. 42)

- Two-minute state check: Breath, long exhale, shoulders down. Intent: "learn fast"
- Map unknowns: "Here are the top three uncertainties"
- Invite challenges: "What am I missing?" Call on low-status voices first
- Surface near-miss: Rotate who shares one caught-late risk

- Credit candor: Record what we'll test. Publicly thank the person who improved the plan
- Run for eight weeks

Chapter 5: Humility Rewired

Celebration of Vulnerability (p. 86)

- Publicly acknowledge when candor improved a decision
- Stories spread safety faster than policies

30-Day Humility Sprint (p. 86)

- Week 1: Two admits rule
- Week 2: Blameless postmortem on a small miss
- Week 3: Junior-first speaking order
- Week 4: Documented "assumptions log" with revisit date
- Debrief on what changed

Measurement: How to Know It's Working (p. 87)

Leading Indicators:

- Number of assumptions logged before decisions
- Count of early escalations (raised risks before incidents)
- Voice distribution (how many unique speakers per meeting; junior-first rates)

Lagging Indicators:

- Rework reduction after postmortems
- Time-to-truth (days from first signal to action)
- Retention of high-potential, historically quiet contributors
- Track for one quarter

Chapter 6: Rewriting the Script

Peer Challenge Partner (p. 106)

- Share one limiting script with a trusted colleague
- Ask them to reflect on the evidence you're overlooking

Team Script Check (p. 106)

- In your next staff meeting, ask: "What's one phrase or belief that holds this team back?"
- Use the moment to begin a collective rewrite

Chapter 7: Centered Leadership

Feedback Ritual (p. 118)

- In tense conversations, begin with: "Here's what I may not see"
- Disarms ego and signals humility

Team Reflection (p. 119)

- End meetings with a centering question: "What truth emerged today that we need to carry forward?"

Chapter 8: Quiet Confidence

Assertive but Humble Scripts (Team Training) (p. 133)

- "I may be wrong, but I'm concerned about..."
- "Can we double-check this step?"
- Train the entire team in these communication protocols

The SBAR Rehearsal (p. 133)

- Situation
- Background
- Assessment
- Recommendation
- Practice until they become natural

Chapter 9: Building Resilient Teams

The Check-In Circle (p. 142)

- Begin meetings with a one-word check-in: "What's your state right now?"
- Lowers cortisol, signals care, normalizes emotion

The Red Team Drill (p. 143)

- Assign a subgroup to challenge assumptions
- Invite critique as a safeguard, not a threat

Blameless Postmortems (p. 143)

- After errors, teams gather to review what happened without finger-pointing
- Reframes error as data, not incompetence

Gratitude Rounds (p. 143)

- At the end of a week, each team member names one contribution from a peer
- Increases oxytocin, builds trust, buffers stress

Assumption Logging (p. 143)

- Teams keep a running log of key assumptions behind decisions
- Review logs to prevent overconfidence

Micro-Recovery Breaks (p. 144)

- 2–5 minutes of stretching, breathing, or walking
- Leaders normalize breaks to reduce fatigue

Daily Check-In (p. 146)

- Begin meetings with one-word emotional states

- Normalize emotion

Feedback Loops (p. 146)

- Adopt after-action reviews after major events
- Leaders admit errors first

Voice Calibration (p. 146)

- Ask the lowest-status person first in discussions
- Breaks hierarchy bias

Gratitude Ritual (p. 146)

- End Fridays with "one thing someone did that helped me this week"

Red Team Rotation (p. 146)

- Rotate who challenges assumptions each week
- Reward dissent that improves plans

Silence Audit (p. 146)

- Track who spoke least in meetings
- Ask them privately what could invite their voice

Assumption Log (p. 146)

- Keep a visible record of key decisions and uncertainties
- Review quarterly

Recovery Practices (p. 147)

- Model breaks, breathwork, and psychological detachment
- Teams mirror what leaders normalize

Emotion Naming (p. 147)

- In tense moments, say what you see: "I sense frustration"
- Lowers threat perception

Celebration of Learning (p. 147)

- End projects by naming what mistakes taught—not just what successes proved

Reflection Prompt #9: Team Resilience Assessment (p. 147)

- Think of your current team
- Where do you see resilience—and where do you see fragility?
- Which ritual could you introduce this month to make humility, clarity, and voice part of the team's fabric?

Chapter 10: The Courage to Decide

Dissent Invitation (p. 161)

- Ask one person to argue against your decision
- Reward their courage

The Empty Chair (p. 161)

- Leave a chair in the room to represent the absent stakeholder (patient, customer, future employee)
- Ask: "What would they say?"

Feedback Forum (p. 161)

- After decisions, debrief not just results but process
- Ask: "What made this easier or harder to decide?"

Chapter 11: Faith, Identity, and Eternal Impact

Mentorship with Generations in Mind (p. 181)

- Shift from "How do I succeed?" to "How do I build successors who thrive after me?"

Legacy Storytelling (p. 184)

- Once a quarter, tell your team a story of someone whose humility shaped you
- Stories carry values deeper than rules

CULTURAL CHANGE INITIATIVES

Chapter 6: Rewriting the Script

Script Reset in Organizations (p. 103)

- Language Audit: Replace fear phrases ("Don't rock the boat") with curiosity-driven alternatives ("What blind spot are we missing?")
- Symbolic Acts: Leaders admitting ignorance, crediting dissent
- Shared Rituals: Blameless postmortems, junior-first speaking orders, democratizing voice through checklists
- Storytelling: Retell moments when humility or candor saved the mission

Chapter 9: Building Resilient Teams

Measurement: How to Know It's Working (p. 87)

Leading Indicators:

- Number of assumptions logged before decisions
- Count of early escalations (raised risks before incidents)
- Voice distribution (how many unique speakers per meeting; junior-first rates)

Lagging Indicators:

- Rework reduction after postmortems
- Time-to-truth (days from first signal to action)
- Retention of high-potential, historically quiet contributors
- Track for one quarter

QUICK REFERENCE: EXERCISES BY TIME COMMITMENT

1-MINUTE PRACTICES

- The Pause-and-Presence Drill (Ch 5)
- Micro-Gratitude Practice (Ch 8)
- Body Scan Reset (Ch 8)
- Non-Reactivity Cue (Ch 7)
- Reframe the Question (Ch 11)

5-MINUTE PRACTICES

- The Command State Breath (Ch 6)
- The 5-Minute Breath Reset (Ch 10)
- The Clarity Script (Ch 8)
- Breath and Prayer Practice (Ch 11)
- The Centering Breath (Ch 7)
- The Eternal Perspective Reset (Ch 11)

10-MINUTE PRACTICES

- Morning Stillness (Ch 12)
- 10-Minute Weekly Team Practice (Ch 2)

DAILY PRACTICES

- Two-Column Journal (Ch 6, 12)
- Daily Gratitude List (Ch 12)
- The Mirror Ritual (Ch 12)

- Daily Self-Check (Ch 5)
- Celebration Journal (Ch 6)
- Daily Detachment (Ch 8)
- Confidence Journal (Ch 8)
- Daily Centering (Ch 7)
- The Daily Integrity Audit (Ch 11)
- Micro-Acts of Service (Ch 11)
- Practice Anonymity (Ch 11)

WEEKLY PRACTICES

- Script Audit (Ch 6)
- Wisdom Journaling (Ch 7)
- Service Audit (Ch 11, 12)
- Journaling for Legacy (Ch 11)
- Weekly Reflection Sabbath (Ch 12)
- Mentor Touchpoint (Ch 12)
- Eternal Scoreboard Review (Ch 11)

MONTHLY/QUARTERLY PRACTICES

- Service Audit (Ch 11)
- Eternal Impact Review (Ch 11)
- Eternity Journal (Ch 11)
- Legacy Storytelling (Ch 11)
- Decision Journal Review (Ch 10)

EXERCISES BY CHAPTER

CHAPTER 1: UNCOVERING THE GOLD WITHIN

Individual:

- Telltale Behaviors Self-Check
- Reflection Prompt #1: Plaster vs. Gold

CHAPTER 2: THE COST OF THE MASK

Individual:

- Leader's Health Red Flags Audit
- Reflection Prompt #2: Earning Your Right

Team:

- 10-Minute Weekly Practice

CHAPTER 3: THE FALSE SELF

Individual:

- Reflection Prompt #3: False Humility Check

CHAPTER 4: UNMASKING THE INNER CRITIC

Individual:

- Reflection Prompt #4: Naming the Distortion

CHAPTER 5: HUMILITY REWIRED

Individual:

- The Pause-and-Presence Drill
- Gratitude Reframe
- Perspective Switch
- Structured Pauses
- The "Two Admits" Rule
- The "Ask-Then-Answer" Turn
- Daily Self-Check
- Trust Audit
- Perspective Practice
- Learning Loop
- Reflection Prompt #5: Reactivity Reframe

Team:

- Celebration of Vulnerability
- 30-Day Humility Sprint

CHAPTER 6: REWRITING THE SCRIPT

Individual:

- The "Two-Column Journal"
- The Command State Breath
- Identity-Based Affirmations
- The Leadership Rehearsal (Focused Visualization)
- Script Audit (Weekly)

- Breath-Anchor Ritual
- Identity Affirmation Card
- Visualization Rehearsal
- Voice Calibration
- Celebration Journal
- Reflection Prompt #6: Script Rewrite

Team:

- Peer Challenge Partner
- Team Script Check
- Script Reset in Organizations

CHAPTER 7: CENTERED LEADERSHIP

Individual:

- The Centering Breath
- The "Wisdom Over Wounds" Journal
- The Non-Reactivity Cue
- Detachment Practice
- Daily Centering
- Wisdom Journaling
- Consistency Audit
- Non-Attachment Check
- Reflection Prompt #7: Triggered by Praise or Blame

Team:

- Feedback Ritual
- Team Reflection

CHAPTER 8: QUIET CONFIDENCE

Individual:

- The Clarity Script
- The Curiosity Cue
- Feedback Reframe
- Body Scan Reset
- Micro-Gratitude Practice
- Posture Check-In
- Presence Audit
- Voice Calibration
- Feedback Ritual
- Posture Practice
- Daily Detachment
- Confidence Journal
- Reflection Prompt #8: Speaking with Quiet Confidence

Team:

- Assertive but Humble Scripts (Team Training)
- The SBAR Rehearsal

CHAPTER 9: BUILDING RESILIENT TEAMS

Team:

- The Check-In Circle
- The Red Team Drill
- Blameless Postmortems
- Gratitude Rounds

- Assumption Logging
- Micro-Recovery Breaks
- Daily Check-In
- Feedback Loops
- Voice Calibration
- Gratitude Ritual
- Red Team Rotation
- Silence Audit
- Assumption Log
- Recovery Practices
- Emotion Naming
- Celebration of Learning
- Reflection Prompt #9: Team Resilience Assessment
- Measurement: How to Know It's Working

CHAPTER 10: THE COURAGE TO DECIDE

Individual:

- The Values Filter
- The Pre-Mortem
- The 70% Rule
- The Three Horizons
- Decision Journal
- The 5-Minute Breath Reset
- Scenario Triad
- Failure Letter
- Reflection Prompt #10: Values-Based Decision

Team:

- Dissent Invitation

- The Empty Chair
- Feedback Forum

CHAPTER 11: FAITH, IDENTITY, AND ETERNAL IMPACT

Individual:

- Redefining Success: A Practical Exercise
- The Daily Integrity Audit
- The 48-Hour Rule
- Reframe the Question
- Build an Eternal Scoreboard
- Practice Anonymity
- Curate Your Inputs
- The Eternal Perspective Reset
- Journaling for Legacy
- Breath and Prayer Practice
- Identity Anchoring Affirmation
- Eternal Time Horizon Exercise
- Service Audit
- Eternal Impact Review
- Micro-Acts of Service
- Prayerful Discernment
- Eternity Journal
- Reflection Prompt #11: Leadership Legacy

Team:

- Mentorship with Generations in Mind
- Legacy Storytelling

CHAPTER 12: THE DAILY PRACTICE OF HUMBLE CONFIDENCE

Individual:

- Morning Stillness (10 minutes)
- The Command State Primer (Breathwork)
- Two-Column Journal
- Daily Gratitude List
- The Mirror Ritual
- Identity Anchor Card
- Weekly Reflection Sabbath
- Mentor Touchpoint
- Service Audit
- Reflection Prompt #12: Ritual Anchor

EXERCISES BY THEME

EGO WORK & SELF-AWARENESS

- Telltale Behaviors Self-Check (Ch 1)
- Leader's Health Red Flags Audit (Ch 2)
- Reflection Prompt #3: False Humility Check (Ch 3)
- Reflection Prompt #4: Naming the Distortion (Ch 4)
- Daily Self-Check (Ch 5)
- Trust Audit (Ch 5)
- Reflection Prompt #5: Reactivity Reframe (Ch 5)
- The "Two-Column Journal" (Ch 6, 12)
- Script Audit (Ch 6)
- Reflection Prompt #6: Script Rewrite (Ch 6)

- The "Wisdom Over Wounds" Journal (Ch 7)
- Detachment Practice (Ch 7)
- Non-Attachment Check (Ch 7)
- Reflection Prompt #7: Triggered by Praise or Blame (Ch 7)
- Daily Detachment (Ch 8)
- Presence Audit (Ch 8)

SUCCESS DEFINITION & VALIDATION

- Redefining Success: A Practical Exercise (Ch 11)
- The Daily Integrity Audit (Ch 11)
- The 48-Hour Rule (Ch 11)
- Reframe the Question (Ch 11)
- Build an Eternal Scoreboard (Ch 11)
- Practice Anonymity (Ch 11)
- Curate Your Inputs (Ch 11)
- The Eternal Perspective Reset (Ch 11)

BREATHWORK & CENTERING

- The Command State Breath (Ch 6)
- Breath-Anchor Ritual (Ch 6)
- The Centering Breath (Ch 7)
- Daily Centering (Ch 7)
- The 5-Minute Breath Reset (Ch 10)
- Breath and Prayer Practice (Ch 11)
- Morning Stillness (Ch 12)
- The Command State Primer (Ch 12)

FEEDBACK PRACTICES

- Gratitude Reframe (Ch 5)
- Structured Pauses (Ch 5)
- The "Two Admits" Rule (Ch 5)
- The "Ask-Then-Answer" Turn (Ch 5)
- Perspective Practice (Ch 5)
- Feedback Reframe (Ch 8)
- Micro-Gratitude Practice (Ch 8)
- Feedback Ritual (Ch 8)
- Feedback Ritual (Team, Ch 7)
- Feedback Loops (Team, Ch 9)
- Dissent Invitation (Team, Ch 10)

IDENTITY & SCRIPT WORK

- Identity-Based Affirmations (Ch 6)
- Identity Affirmation Card (Ch 6)
- The Leadership Rehearsal (Ch 6)
- Visualization Rehearsal (Ch 6)
- Celebration Journal (Ch 6)
- Identity Anchoring Affirmation (Ch 11)
- The Mirror Ritual (Ch 12)
- Identity Anchor Card (Ch 12)

VOICE & COMMUNICATION

- Voice Calibration (Ch 6, 8)
- The Clarity Script (Ch 8)
- The Curiosity Cue (Ch 8)
- Posture Check-In (Ch 8)
- Posture Practice (Ch 8)

- Confidence Journal (Ch 8)
- Reflection Prompt #8: Speaking with Quiet Confidence (Ch 8)
- Assertive but Humble Scripts (Team, Ch 8)
- The SBAR Rehearsal (Team, Ch 8)

DECISION-MAKING

- The Values Filter (Ch 10)
- The Pre-Mortem (Ch 10)
- The 70% Rule (Ch 10)
- The Three Horizons (Ch 10)
- Decision Journal (Ch 10)
- Scenario Triad (Ch 10)
- Failure Letter (Ch 10)
- Reflection Prompt #10: Values-Based Decision (Ch 10)
- Prayerful Discernment (Ch 11)
- Eternal Time Horizon Exercise (Ch 11)

LEGACY & SERVICE

- Journaling for Legacy (Ch 11)
- Service Audit (Ch 11, 12)
- Eternal Impact Review (Ch 11)
- Micro-Acts of Service (Ch 11)
- Eternity Journal (Ch 11)
- Reflection Prompt #11: Leadership Legacy (Ch 11)
- Legacy Storytelling (Team, Ch 11)

TEAM BUILDING

- 10-Minute Weekly Practice (Ch 2)
- Celebration of Vulnerability (Ch 5)
- 30-Day Humility Sprint (Ch 5)
- Peer Challenge Partner (Ch 6)
- Team Script Check (Ch 6)
- Team Reflection (Ch 7)
- The Check-In Circle (Ch 9)
- The Red Team Drill (Ch 9)
- Blameless Postmortems (Ch 9)
- Gratitude Rounds (Ch 9)
- Assumption Logging (Ch 9)
- All other Chapter 9 team practices

CONSISTENCY BUILDING

- The Pause-and-Presence Drill (Ch 5)
- The Non-Reactivity Cue (Ch 7)
- Consistency Audit (Ch 7)
- Body Scan Reset (Ch 8)
- Weekly Reflection Sabbath (Ch 12)
- Mentor Touchpoint (Ch 12)
- Reflection Prompt #12: Ritual Anchor (Ch 12)

RECOMMENDED PATHWAYS

THE FOCUSED PATH (90 Days)

- Pick 5-7 exercises that address your most urgent growth edge:
- Week 1-4: Choose one breathwork practice + one daily journal
- Week 5-8: Add one feedback practice + one team ritual
- Week 9-12: Incorporate one legacy practice + review all

THE DEEP DIVE (One Quarter)

- Choose exercises from a single theme and become exceptional in that domain:
- Example—Ego Work: Complete all ego work exercises over 12 weeks
- Example—Decision-Making: Master all decision tools over 12 weeks

THE TEAM CURRICULUM

Select exercises designed for group reflection:

- Month 1: Team safety and voice (Ch 2, 5, 9)
- Month 2: Feedback and decision culture (Ch 7, 8, 10)
- Month 3: Legacy and service orientation (Ch 11)

THE INTUITIVE APPROACH

Read straight through, try whatever resonates in the moment. Reference this appendix later when ready for more structured practice.

APPENDIX B: QR Codes

Join our Skool Community

Schedule a one on one

Take the Humility Assessment - Free

Citations

CHAPTER 1: UNCOVERING THE GOLD WITHIN (IMPOSTER SYNDROME)

- Bravata, D. M., et al. (2020). Prevalence, predictors, and treatment of imposter syndrome: A systematic review. *Journal of General Internal Medicine*, 35(4), 1252-1275.

- Edmondson, A. (1999). Psychological safety and learning behavior in work teams. *Administrative Science Quarterly*, 44(2), 350-383.

- Koven, S. (2016). Letter to a young female physician. *New England Journal of Medicine*, 374, 1907-1909.

- Journal of Vocational Behavior. (2021). Imposter syndrome and underrepresented minorities: Effects on career motivation and planning, 58(1), 1–11.

- Miao, C., Humphrey, R. H., & Qian, S. (2018). Emotional intelligence and team performance: A meta-analysis. *Journal of Organizational Behavior*, 39(2), 242-256.

- Goyal, M., et al. (2014). Meditation programs for psychological stress and well-being: A systematic review and meta-analysis. *JAMA Internal Medicine*, 174(3), 357–368.

- Hölzel, B. K., et al. (2011). Mindfulness practice leads to increases in regional brain gray matter density. *Psychiatry Research: Neuroimaging*, 191(1), 36-43.

CHAPTER 2: THE COST OF THE MASK

- Bravata, D. M., et al. (2020). Prevalence ... (as above).

Citations

- Shanafelt, T. D., et al. (2015). Impostor phenomenon in US physicians relative to burnout and professional fulfillment. *Mayo Clinic Proceedings*, 90(11), 1615-1623.

- Frontiers in Psychology. (2019). Imposter syndrome and leadership motivation, 10, 2113.

- Blind. (2018). Survey of tech professionals on imposter syndrome.

- Smith, M. M., et al. (2016). Perfectionism and burnout: A meta-analysis. *Journal of Vocational Behavior*, 92, 155–167.

- Schultz, H. (2011). *Onward: How Starbucks Fought for Its Life without Losing Its Soul*. New York, NY: Rodale.

- Edmondson, A. (1999). Psychological safety ... (as above).

- Journal of Vocational Behavior. (2021). Imposter feelings & career planning (as above).

- U.S. Army, After-Action Review (AAR) practice.

CHAPTER 3: THE FALSE SELF

- Moran, J. M., et al. (2014). Neuroanatomical evidence for distinct cognitive operations during self-reflection. *Social Cognitive and Affective Neuroscience*, 9(6), 744-749.

- Stoic texts: Epictetus, *Discourses*; Marcus Aurelius, *Meditations*.

- Lam, J., et al. (2018). Humblebragging: Misguided attempts at self-promotion. *Journal of Applied Psychology*, 103(7), 778-795.

- BMJ Quality & Safety. (2014). Surgical trainee case study.

CHAPTER 4: UNMASKING THE INNER CRITIC

- Frost, R. O., & Marten, P. (1990). Perfectionism and self-critical thinking. *Journal of Personality and Social Psychology*, 58(5), 878–892.

- Mindfulness and Rumination: Farb, N. A., et al. (2010). Attending to the present: Mindfulness meditation reveals distinct neural modes of self-reference. *Social Cognitive and Affective Neuroscience*, 5(1), 35-43.

- Jazaieri, H., et al. (2014). Default Mode Network activity in mindfulness: Self vs. other reference. *Mindfulness*, 5(1), 72–79.

- Medial prefrontal cortex and identity: Moran, J. M., et al. (2014). (as above).

- Brauer, M., et al. (2016). Attribution reframing in imposter syndrome. *Journal of Counseling Psychology*, 63(4), 485–494.

CHAPTER 5: HUMILITY REWIRED

- Moran, J. M., et al. (2014). (as above).

- Zak, P. J. (2017). The neuroscience of trust. *Harvard Business Review*, 95(1), 84-90.

- BMJ Leader. (2021). Humility, trust, psychological safety in medicine, 5(1), 1-7.

- Miao, C., Humphrey, R. H., & Qian, S. (2018). (as above).

- Goyal, M., et al. (2014). (as above).

- Case: Michigan Keystone ICU Project.

CHAPTER 6: REWRITING THE SCRIPT

- Brauer, M., et al. (2016). (as above).

- Goodman, D., et al. (2005). Critical care team dynamics and hierarchy. *Critical Care Medicine*, 33(8), 1643–1649.

- Sherman, D. K., et al. (2013). Affirmations and stress reduction. *Personality and Social Psychology Bulletin*, 39(5), 637-650.

- Google, Mindfulness Leadership training.

- Schultz, H. (2011). (as above).

CHAPTER 7: CENTERED LEADERSHIP

- Zhu, Z., et al. (2021). Admitting limits and humility in leaders. *Organizational Behavior and Human Decision Processes*, 163, 71-89.

- Owens, B. P., & Hekman, D. R. (2012). (as above).

- Rego, A., et al. (2021). Humble leadership and ethical voice. *Journal of Business Ethics*, 170, 935–952.

- Cummings, G. G., et al. (2021). Calm leadership and burnout in healthcare. *BMJ Open*, 11, e054983.

- Leadership Quarterly. (2017). Leader behavior and trust.

- Story: James Mattis, U.S. Secretary of Defense—*Call Sign Chaos*. New York, NY: Random House.

CHAPTER 8: QUIET CONFIDENCE

- Cuddy, A. J., et al. (2015). Presence: Bringing your boldest self. *Harvard Business Review*, 93(12), 90-98.

Citations

- Owens, B. P., & Hekman, D. R. (2012). (as above).

- International Journal of Research in Marketing. (2013). Crossed arms and negotiation.

- MIT Sloan Management Review. (2019). Leader openness.

- Lincoln, A., et al., Roosevelt, F. D., Mandela, N.—Historical examples.

- Emotion. (2018). Leadership presence and posture.

- BMJ Leader. (2022). Humility and team outcomes (as above).

CHAPTER 9: BUILDING RESILIENT TEAMS WITH EMOTIONAL CLARITY

- Owens, B. P., & Hekman, D. R. (2012). (as above).

- Cummings, G. G., et al. (2021). Humble leadership and nurse turnover (as above).

- Harvard Business Review. (2019). Emotional check-ins and group cohesion.

- Nature Human Behaviour. (2021). Prioritization and cognitive bandwidth.

- Occupational Health Science. (2016). Micro-breaks and team engagement.

- Case: Google Project Aristotle.

CHAPTER 10: THE COURAGE TO DECIDE—HOW HUMILITY FUELS BOLD DECISIONS

- Baumeister, R. F., et al. (2007). The strength model of self-control. *Current Directions in Psychological Science*, 16(6), 351-355.

- Danziger, S., et al. (2011). Extraneous factors in judicial decisions. *Proceedings of the National Academy of Sciences*, 108(17), 6889–6892.

- Frontiers in Psychology. (2018). Decision paralysis and negative evaluation.

- BMJ Quality & Safety. (2015). Delay and hierarchy in medical emergencies.

- Historical/Philosophy: Epictetus, Dhammapada, *Holy Bible*, Proverbs 11:2.

CHAPTER 11: FAITH, IDENTITY, AND ETERNAL IMPACT

- Journal of Behavioral Science. (2019). Success definitions and imposter syndrome.

- Marcus Aurelius. *Meditations*.

- Epictetus. *Discourses*.

- The Holy Bible. Matthew 5, Proverbs 11:2, Galatians 1:10.

- The Qur'an 28:77. Bhagavad Gita 2:47.

- Brauer, M., et al. (2016). (as above).

- Collins, J. (2001). *Good to Great*. New York, NY: HarperBusiness.

Citations

- Florence Nightingale—Biography.

- Good to Great—Jim Collins.

- Washington, G., Mandela, N., Tutu, D.—Biographical references.

CHAPTER 12: THE DAILY PRACTICE OF HUMBLE CONFIDENCE

- Jazaieri, H., et al. (2016). Daily reflection and leader resilience. *Journal of Applied Psychology*, 101(1), 38–49.

- Neff, K. D. (2011). (as above).

- Frontiers in Psychology. (2017). Breathwork and HRV.

- Phelps, M.—Biography (Olympic athlete, practices).

- Personality and Individual Differences. (2017). Daily gratitude and leadership perception.

- Organizational Behavior and Human Decision Processes. (2016). Ritual and performance.

- Journal of the American College of Surgeons. (2018). Paced breathing in surgery.

- Gandhi—Biography.

- Jensen Huang—Biography.

APPENDICES / FURTHER READING

- Edmondson, A., Collins, J., Greenleaf, R. K., Goleman, D., Stoic and Buddhist texts, and others referenced above.

About the Author

J. Alexander is a John Maxwell speaker, coach, and trainer and a Maxwell DISC Certified consultant who helps high-performing professionals lead with confidence, emotional intelligence, and humility—especially under pressure. A Marine Corps veteran and faith-driven entrepreneur, J. blends neuroscience, real-world leadership experience, and practical inner-work to address imposter syndrome, burnout, and the quiet inner battles many leaders face.

He is the founder of Excelerate You Coaching and the creator of the Humility Advantage™ framework, working primarily with healthcare executives and high-stress leadership teams. Known for his direct yet compassionate style, J. challenges leaders to shed false personas, build psychological safety, and lead from a grounded, authentic center.

J. lives with his wife, Holly, and the parents of five children with eight grandchildren and growing. When he's not coaching or writing, he's focused on disciplined daily practices, lifelong growth, and helping leaders create impact that lasts beyond their title.

THE HUMILITY ADVANTAGE IN ACTION

Coming in 2027

Leading Beyond Yourself

J. ALEXANDER

Made in the USA
Coppell, TX
04 March 2026

72912951R10164